ARROW FAMILY HANDBOOK

TIME OUT TOGETHER

D1740246

Arrow Family Handbooks

In any family's life there are bound to be major turning points, choices or moments of decision. Arrow Family Handbooks are designed to explore the alternatives and provide the information and practical advice you need.

Series editor: Mary Gilliatt.

Other titles already published in this series:

Setting Up Home
A basic guide to what you need
Mary Gilliatt

Making Ends Meet
A practical guide to family finance
Elizabeth Gundrey

Growing Up
A practical guide to adolescence for parents and children
Catherine Storr

Time Out Together

A practical guide to family leisure
out of doors

CAROLINE MACKINLAY

Arrow Books

Arrow Books Limited
3 Fitzroy Square, London W1

An imprint of the Hutchinson Publishing Group

London Melbourne Sydney Auckland
Wellington Johannesburg and agencies
throughout the world

First published by Arrow Books Ltd 1975
© Caroline Mackinlay 1975

Made and printed in Great Britain
by The Anchor Press Ltd
Tiptree, Essex

ISBN 0 09 911300 7

Contents

Equipment
Holiday Courses

PART II - WHERE TO DO WHAT – OUTDOOR
ACTIVITIES IN THE NATIONAL PARKS

Information Centres
Motoring
Day Outings and Weekends
Further Reference

7. North York Moors National Park

Walking
Angling
Gliding
Swimming
Pony Trekking and Riding
Archaeology
Geology
Accommodation
Books
Information Centres
Day Outings and Weekends

8. Peak District

Walking, Riding and Pony Trekking
Rock Climbing
Caving and Potholing
Archaeology
Geology
Angling
Birdwatching
Canoeing
Holiday Centre
Camping and Caravanning
Information Centre
Day Outings and Weekends

9. Pembrokeshire Coast

Walking
Pony Trekking
Angling
Sailing
Swimming
Sub-Aqua Swimming
Gliding
Birdwatching
Sea Life
Archaeology
Geology

Part I. Taking Up New Activities

How to use this book

The object of this book is to introduce families to the many different possibilities of active holidays, more enterprising than a week at the seaside, pleasant though that can be; holidays which will, perhaps, enlarge the scope of living and the areas of observation, which will spark off new interests in both parents and children and introduce them to hobbies which could last a lifetime.

The first section of the book is about how to take up activities which are new to you – from angling to underwater swimming – and the second section describes the countryside where you can practise them, the National Parks. The assumption is that families on holiday, whether for a week or a weekend, don't necessarily always do everything together – one may want to go pony trekking while the others are hill walking.

The intelligent use of leisure in the coming years will be the key to the happiness and creativity of most people in Britain. As more and more leisure hours become available we shall have to find worthwhile activities to fill them with, and places where we can practise them. The National Parks are already making it possible for thousands of people to enjoy their leisure in unspoiled countryside. And it is now up to people to see that these beautiful areas remain unspoiled.

Prices: I have quoted prices so as to give you an idea of *approximate cost*. Though correct at the time of going to press, I must warn readers that, owing to inflation, prices may no longer be accurate.

1. Angling

Different Types of Angling. Angling Clubs. Courses. Children. Publications. Permits. Equipment.

DIFFERENT TYPES OF ANGLING

Today, according to a recent survey, more people go fishing at weekends than watch professional football. If you are thinking of taking up angling you probably already have a predilection for one particular branch of the sport. There are three varieties, all very different in character and appeal.

Sea Angling. This is done from a boat, a pier, a beach or even rocks, is active and exciting and introduces you to many different kinds of fish and often plenty of them. They vary in size from the small flat dab to the huge cod, and in character from the elusive hard-to-get mullet, to the impulsive fighting mackerel. (Fishing all year, no close season.)

Coarse Fishing. On rivers and lakes, from the bank or from a boat, a placid and friendly pursuit, coarse fishing is frequently done in groups of two or three and it also offers you a variety of fish, from the roach, chub, dace class, to the large pike and carp. (Season from 16 June to 15 March.)

Game Fishing. Fishing for trout and salmon, usually with the fly, is regarded by those who do it as an art and as quite the most elegant, esoteric way of catching fish. (The season varies considerably in different areas, but generally speaking, it runs from 1 April to 30 September.)

ANGLING CLUBS

The easiest and probably the most satisfactory way of learning whichever branch of angling you take up, is to join a reputable angling club of which there are thousands throughout the country. You can find out what is available in your area by writing to the relevant body: on *sea angling*, the National Federation of Sea Anglers, 26 Downsview Cresent, Uckfield, Sussex TN22 1UB, will give advice; on *coarse fishing*, the National Federation of Anglers, Haig House, 87 Green Lane, Derby; on *trout and salmon fishing*, The Salmon & Trout Association, Fishmongers' Hall, London EC4R 9EL.

COURSES

These bodies are affiliated to the National Anglers' Council (address below), under whose auspices a National Coaching Scheme is now running. This provides, with the co-operation of the National Federation of Anglers, coarse fishing instructors in most parts of the country, who hold courses and who can be contacted through the Council.

CHILDREN

Courses in all types of angling are run in most areas of England by Education Authorities and/or Sports Councils and you can get detailed lists from the National Anglers' Council (address below). Children are accepted on most of these courses though the starting ages differ. Some areas run a Junior Basic Angling course for boys and girls, in which starting ages vary from eight, to ten, to twelve. Coarse fishing holidays for boys of eleven to fifteen are organized yearly by the Youth Hostels Association, Trevelyan House, St Albans, Hertfordshire AL1 2DY. Information on all types of fishing courses, book lists, angling film lists and other informative leaflets can be got through the National Anglers' Council, 17 Queen Street, Peterborough PE1 1PJ.

The Salmon & Trout Association run two or three fly fishing courses a year for boys and girls from twelve to eighteen, children of members. For details of membership write to the Association, address as above. There are many instruction and holiday courses run by private individuals and advertised in the fishing magazines, in particular, the *Trout and Salmon* magazine.

PUBLICATIONS

Two authoritative weekly newspapers are useful sources of help and information: *Anglers' Mail*, based in London, tends to cover the south, and *Angling Times* in Peterborough to serve the Midlands. Both carry informative articles helpful to the beginner. The *Sheffield Telegraph* produces special angling features and a supplement – The *Angling Telegraph*. There are also several magazines and innumerable books.

Where to Fish by Dick Orton, published every other year by the *Field*, is a comprehensive and very detailed guide to what fishing, of every kind, is available. Entries come under the headings of rivers and their tributaries and include rivers, lakes, lochs and reservoirs in England, Wales, Scotland and Northern Ireland; they describe the kind of fishing, the tickets and permits necessary, as well as prices and close seasons. It is an invaluable source of information and available in most public libraries.

PERMITS

Since there is practically no free fishing in Britain except on the Thames below Staines, it is almost always imperative that you get (a) a licence to fish from the appropriate River Authority and (b) a permit from the owner of the river bank, who owns the water up to the middle of the river. Where a club is the owner you must either join it or get a day/weekly ticket. Information about who owns different stretches of river can be obtained from *Where to Fish*, the publication mentioned above.

The sea is free for all but not necessarily the shore which, above the mean high water mark, probably belongs to someone and you may have to get permission for access.

Close seasons are defined by the local River Authority but are roughly the same throughout the country. The sea has no close season.

EQUIPMENT

Coarse Fishing. (Freshwater fish other than salmon, trout and grayling.)

Equipment: rod, reel, line and accessories.
The choice of rod depends very much on the kind of fish you are going after, for unfortunately there is no such thing as an all-purpose rod. It is important to take advice on what rod you buy because your success depends on its being right for the job. An experienced angler could guide you, or a reputable tackle dealer. (It is not usually possible to hire equipment.)

There are several kinds of reel and again the choice is dependent on the sort of fishing you intend to do, so get advice if you can.

You will also hopefully need a landing net and a keep net in which to place the live fish.

Clothes: Rubber boots are essential and any tough, warm clothes suitably weatherproofed.

Game Fishing. (Salmon, sea trout also known as migratory trout and as sewin, brown trout, rainbow trout, grayling.)

Equipment: Rod, reel, line, cast, flies and accessories.

Trout. The choice of rod depends on the kind of water

you intend to fish and this is closely related to the area you choose. For example, boat fishing from a loch in Scotland will require a different rod from fishing a small-ish river in the West Country, so first decide on the kind of water you intend to fish before selecting a rod.

Prices of trout rods do in fact reflect craftsmanship so you get the quality you pay for. You will also need line, casts, flies (artificial) and a landing net. A good rod needs the right reel, line, cast and fly, so take expert advice before you buy. An angling friend or a dealer may help you. *Rainbow trout*, imported years ago from America, respond to much the same tackle as the indigenous brown trout. Ordinary trout tackle is also suitable for *sea trout* fishing, unless the trout are expected to exceed 8 lb, when heavier tackle would be more effective.

Grayling.   Are at their best in the autumn and early winter just as the trout season closes. Tackle is in general the same as for trout.

Salmon.   What salmon rod you buy depends largely on how much you intend to spend and how much and where you are going to fish. Rods are made of steel or split-cane or fibreglass. It is now generally agreed that 'glass' rods, which are very much cheaper, are almost as good as cane, and certainly excellent for the beginner. Again, it is im-portant to get advice from an expert on the rod, reel and line you are going to use. It is particularly essential that the line and reel are right for the rod.

Clothes: Generally speaking, rubber boots, waterproof trousers, jacket and hat; for salmon, thigh-length or chest-length waders.

Accessories: Landing net and gaff.

Sea Angling.   Equipment: rod, reel, line and accessories. In sea angling, as in coarse fishing, your choice of rod depends on the type of fishing you intend to do, i.e.

18   whether it is from a boat, a beach, or a pier. Try to consult an expert before you buy.

Accessories: Lead weights, hooks and terminal tackle; landing nets and gaffs. (When fishing from a boat it is often possible to hire equipment from the boatman.)

Clothes: Sea fishing demands very warm clothing whatever the time of year. For winter, dedicated sea anglers wear a wet-suit together with leather boots.

2. Ballooning

How to Find Out.   How to Learn.   Other Equipment.
A Family Pursuit.   Books.

Hot air ballooning is an escapist thing – getting away from it
all in a rather rare sort of way. It is usually a very tranquil
pursuit. Nothing quite matches the euphoria you can get
when you have time to look down and appreciate the pattern
a tree's branches make, and as well as the tranquillity there
is sometimes excitement – and a satisfying sense of achievement when you land safely.
Roger Barrett, *Chairman of The British Balloon and Airship
Club*

HOW TO FIND OUT

If you are attracted to lighter-than-air activities you can

find out all about them by joining the British Balloon and Airship Club. Annual subscription is £3·00 and £1·00 for juniors under eighteen. The club is open to all interested in flying and application forms can be had from the Membership Secretary, BBAC, Kimberley House, Vaughan Way, Leicester. Membership covers regular social and technical meetings during the winter, plus a copy of the bi-monthly journal the *Aerostat* which will keep you in touch with all ballooning activities. The club undertakes to give you advice and access to information on insurance, Government regulations on licensing and airworthiness, etc.

Training. Pilots have to fly at least twelve hours in a balloon, undergo a medical examination and pass theory examinations on meteorology, air law and ballooning techniques in order to get a licence. He/she must also be seventeen or over. Twelve hours is the legal minimum but most students are ready to go solo around the fifteen-hour mark.

The difference between hot air and gas ballooning is noise. Gas ballooning is silent, hot air ballooning is noisy. A hot air balloon with a lower lifting capacity than gas, costs a few pounds for fuel for one day's flying; but to fill a hydrogen balloon of say 25000 cubic feet will cost up to £200, so I, for obvious reasons, deal here with hot air ballooning.

Today's hot air balloons bear very little relation to the early versions. The fabric now is usually nylon, the fuel is propane and an average volume is 60000 cubic feet. The basket is usually of the conventional kind and flying is achieved by turning the burner on and off, so altering the temperature of the enclosed air, and thereby changing altitude.

HOW TO LEARN

How do you learn without a balloon? One way is to chip

in on a syndicate or group already owning a balloon and share costs and flying time. You can get a list of operators from the BBAC and it is quite possible that a group might welcome a new member. *Or*, you can help to start a syndicate, usually with four to ten members together with others whose names you can get from the BBAC. Once the balloon situation is solved you then persuade a licensed pilot to instruct you. *Or* you can take a full course of instruction at a balloon school, for example, The Europa Balloon School, 344 Wanstead Park Road, Ilford, Essex IG1 3TY.

If you form a syndicate, you must then buy your hot air balloon which will cost you around £2000 fully equipped. There are three manufacturers in the UK, some of whom, incidentally, offer instruction when the order for a balloon is placed and some will also give test flights to serious syndicates. Maintenance will cost around £100 p.a. and insurance ranges from £40 p.a. for third party only, for £50000 cover, to £120 or so for fully comprehensive cover for a balloon valued at £1600. Propane gas prices vary between 1p and 5p per lb depending on the amount bought. One flight with three cylinders will use up to 90 lbs of propane; with four cylinders up to 125 lbs. The average flight lasts from one-and-a-half to two hours.

OTHER EQUIPMENT

You must have a retrieve trailer: professionally built they cost around £100 to £120, or do-it-yourself cost about £50 to £75 and a lot of time.

If you cannot afford it, try attaching yourself to a group that is already flying a balloon. They may welcome your help.

A FAMILY PURSUIT

Is ballooning a family pursuit? That rather depends on

the family. If they are the kind that do not mind getting up at 6 or 7 a.m. (early morning is the best ballooning time) – fine. But they have to be prepared for disappointments, for changes in weather and wind often prevent takeoff.

On the other hand a balloon has to have a crew and there is room for two adults and two children (there is no official minimum age for child passengers) in most baskets, and that makes a fine crew.

BOOKS

Meteorology for Glider Pilots, by C. E. Wallington, John Murray, £3·00. See pages 108–33 and 149–239, which are particularly relevant to ballooning.

To get the feel of ballooning, the fun, the fear and the enchantment read *The Dangerous Sort*, by Anthony Smith, George Allen & Unwin, £2·50.

The First Five Years edited by Anthony Smith, includes technical advice and flying hints, plus stories of balloon flights all culled from early issues of the BBAC's magazine in the late 1960s. It is available from the BBAC (address above) price £2·25.

3. Canal and River Cruising

How to Learn.   The Kind of Boat.   Hiring.
Where to Go.   Clothes.

Canal or river cruising can be the ideal holiday for a family with young children because it has all the right ingredients: a home that is always on the move – at not more than 4 mph on canals – past new scenery, an exciting place to sleep, a boat to help steer, lots of things to do aboard and on shore.

HOW TO LEARN

The best way is to hire a boat for a week or a fortnight.

The hire firm will give you a trial run to explain the works and a brochure with clear instructions. They are as interested as you are that you enjoy your holiday and bring the boat back intact. Bookings start and end on Saturdays.

It is a good idea to read something on the subject before you start, to familiarize yourself with the scene – locks, lifts, tunnels, aqueducts, bridges, towpaths, moorings. *Holiday Cruising on Inland Waterways*, by Charles Hadfield and Michael Streat, gives you a very good start and deals with problems like weed round the prop, going aground, high winds, collisions etc., as well as giving you the basic know-how on taking a motor cruiser on a canal. You can get the book direct from Inland Waterways Association, 114 Regents Park Road, London NW1 8UQ, for 40p, postage 10p. It is also available from libraries.

There is no great skill involved in canal cruising; it is mostly a matter of experience. Going through a lock is puzzling the first time, particularly if there is no lock-keeper, but by the end of the first day or the third lock you will regard yourself as an old hand. If you have a large boat it would help to have one experienced crew member.

THE KIND OF BOAT

Boats vary from small fibreglass cruisers to modern canal cruisers with steel hulls. These are built on the lines of the traditional seventy-foot narrow boats but are shorter and more manoeuvrable. Most boats for hire are equipped with a refrigerator and a cooker. For areas like the Broads and for tidal estuaries, cabin cruisers are used, since canal-type boats are unsuitable. But there is no need to worry as hire firms will only rent you boats suitable for local conditions.

There are hundreds of hire firms around the country and you can get a booklet, 'Waterway Users' Companion', for 45p, plus 12p postage, which gives their names and addresses, from the British Waterways Board, Melbury House, Melbury Terrace, London NW1 6JX. Another list is issued by the Association of Pleasure Craft Operators, 26 Chaseview Road, Alrewas, Burton on Trent, Staffordshire DE13 7EL, describing the holidays offered by their member firms.

The British Waterways Board have two hire bases of their own at Nantwich, Cheshire and Hillmorton near Rugby, Warwickshire. A fully-fitted six-berth canal cruiser hired from them would cost from £114 to £124 a week in March, while a six-berth cruiser in July or August would be around £130 to £160. Cost of hiring should include ship's gear, bedding, cooking, eating and cleaning equipment. Safety equipment is provided. A good time to go is April or May, when not only is the countryside beautifully green, but you get the boat freshly fitted out straight from the yard.

It is essential to take a basic chart of the waterway with you and there are four official guides available by areas: South East, South West, North East and North West. They cost 75p (except for South East which is £1·00) from British Waterways Board in London, address as above, and other regional offices, also by post (postage 20p) from British Waterways Board, Willow Grange, Church Road, Watford WD1 3QA. They are packed full of fascinating and necessary information, from detailed charts to rules of the road and descriptions of the wild life. For the Broads and the Thames the guides are, *The Broads Book*, Link House Publications, price 75p, and *The Thames Book*, Link House Publications, price 75p, both available from Inland Waterways Association (address p. 24).

WHERE TO GO

This depends largely on where you live but there are broadly three choices: the *Thames* from Teddington to Lechlade, which runs through beautiful country with sophisticated waterside pubs, hotels etc. and considerable river traffic. There are forty-three locks in about 120 miles, most of them charmingly laid out with gardens, and often a lock-keeper to give you advice. The *Broads*, Norfolk, where there are no locks, just miles of open water; many waterside facilities, lots of people and easy cruising past wonderful landscape. Or, the *Canal System* – the network of canals all over the country which is harder work because there are no lock-keepers and you must work the locks yourself which, of course, is half the fun. Country pubs are quiet and retiring. No dance halls or waterside hotels and you can cruise all day and meet only one or two craft.

CLOTHES

All children should wear life-jackets, which are mostly provided free by the hire firm. So should all non-swimmers. Clothes should be warm and waterproof and extra clothes are necessary – someone is bound to fall in some time; rubber or rope-soled shoes and a hat against sun or rain.

If you become a canal enthusiast you may want to join the Inland Waterways Association, a voluntary society which continues to play a vital part in keeping canals open and available for all kinds of leisure activities. The annual fee of £4·00 includes a quarterly magazine and access to regional branches. They also publish *Inland Waterways Guide*, price 50p plus 15p postage, available from the Association (address p. 24).

4. Canoeing

How to Learn.   Books.   Equipment.   Clothes.

Canoeing is something you do in groups of about three canoes, and many families canoe in convoy. Once you have learned the elementary principles you will have a choice of taking up racing canoeing, surf canoeing, inland touring or coastal touring – and other variations of the sport. If you go in for inland touring, your canoe will take you into all kinds of beautiful country, and camping by night on the bank (with permission of the owner) in the deep quiet of the country can be unbeatably romantic. You can also get a list of camping sites near waterways from the British Waterways Board, Melbury House, Melbury Terrace, London NW1 6JX. On the sea, life is rougher and only the experienced and highly skilled will attempt coastal touring.

HOW TO LEARN

For several reasons – as you will see – it is a good idea to join a club, and the British Canoe Union, 70 Brompton Road, London SW3 1DT, which is the governing body of the sport, has 400 clubs throughout the country. You can either join one of these or else join the BCU direct. Full membership costs £2·50 a year while under-eighteens pay £1·50. Members whose wives/husbands or children are interested can enrol them for 50p per year each and they have all the privileges of full members except voting rights.

It is essential to be able to swim before taking up canoeing. Weirs and bridges are black spots and beginners should not attempt to approach them alone. Life-jackets should be worn.

The British Canoe Union has a coaching scheme available to members; it also publishes a series of pamphlets on canoeing techniques.

BOOKS

Another advantage of belonging to a club is the availability of advice about where you may or may not canoe and the rights of access to water. The BCU has published a *Guide to Waterways of the British Isles* for the use of its members.

Two useful books for the beginner are *Living Canoeing*, by Alan Byde, A. & C. Black, £2·75, and *Canoeing Complete*, edited by Brian Skilling, Kay & Ward. They are both available in public libraries.

EQUIPMENT

There are many shapes of canoe and which you choose

depends on the kind of canoeing you are going to do; you cannot use the same canoe for all types of canoeing. This is too intricate a problem to go into here, but for general use the beginner will probably buy a glassfibre boat which would cost around £60 already assembled; a kit which you assemble yourself costs from £30. You can buy the canoe direct from specialist manufacturers, and the BCU publish a list of them, available on request.

You will also need paddles, of wood or fibreglass – which cost from £4 each; a spray deck or waterproof cover, also from £4, and a life-jacket from £9.

CLOTHES

Light rubber-soled shoes or sandals, a warm shirt, shorts and a waterproof jacket.

Transport overland has to be by car. If you haven't one, it is said by young members of the BCU to be reasonably easy to get a lift.

There are innumerable canoeing holidays and holiday courses run by Sports Councils and private people, youth clubs and centres all over the country. For details of these see *Activity Holidays*, published at 60p plus 10p postage, by the English Tourist Board, 4 Grosvenor Gardens, London SW1W 0DU.

5. Caving

Why Do It?   How to Learn.   Equipment.

If you are interested in exploring the great underground, then caving and potholing ('caves' are natural underground passages and 'potholes' have steep shafts which require ladders) offer you a vast field of still undiscovered territory . . . but you must be prepared for tough conditions.

Caving, according to cavers Donald Robinson and Anthony Greenbank, 'involves you in darkness, wetness, mud, cold; possibly too for the experienced caver, long, low, tight, wet crawls. Deep pools, canals and lakes. Crevices, pits, slits, shafts, windows and letter-boxes. . . .'

WHY DO IT?

For the beginner a sense of achievement, of facing danger, of working together as a team, of taking part in a sport which tests strength, endurance and courage. You learn new techniques, practically a new language, almost a new way of life.

For the experienced, the explorer's reward of discovering what lies beyond, of finding new caves, new extensions, even new systems to add to the underground map.

And for all who venture underground there is the breathtaking beauty of the caves, all the weird and strangely beautiful formations which go to make up the subterranean scene.

Caving has the reputation of being difficult and dangerous and so it is important to see that you get the right equipment because 'safety precautions alone', as the experts point out, 'are worth little if the equipment is faulty.' You must also be in good physical shape.

The way to start is to join one of the established clubs in one of the four major caving areas. These are to be found in *Derbyshire*'s Peak District, where you get every kind of cave within a few miles of Castleton, the National Park's key point; *Yorkshire*, which has fourteen main caving areas with more than 500 classified potholes and caves; *South Wales*, which has a great variety of caves, and *Mendip*, one of the main caving areas. There is also caving in *Devon*, centred on Buckfastleigh and the Pengelly Research Centre. *The Descent Handbook*, price 50p, from 30 Drake's Road, Wells, Somerset, gives you the names and addresses of all clubs, plus cave surveys, accommodation near caves and other useful information. Or you can get the name and address of your nearest club from the governing body, The National Caving Association, Mrs J. Potts – Secretary, 3 Greenway, Hulland Ward, Derby, who will also provide a list of courses available. The National Scout Caving Centre at Whernside Manor, Dent, via Sedbergh, Cumbria, runs caving courses for all levels of proficiency and will accept people outside the Scout Movement; age sixteen plus, except for weekend caving courses when it is fourteen plus. Details from the above address. *Activity Holidays in England*, price 60p plus 10p postage, from English Tourist Board, 4 Grosvenor Gardens, London SW1W 0DU, also lists available courses under regions.

Unless you live in a caving area it would be wise to join a club with facilities for overnight accommodation. Charges are reasonable and your modest annual subscription probably includes the cost of all caving activities undertaken with them. Most clubs will not accept as *full* members children under sixteen, although much younger children do go caving with enthusiast parents.

EQUIPMENT

You will need a caving helmet, light but strong. It is best to get one with the BSI 'Kite' mark which is proof of quality. Since the caves are completely dark, except in the tourist areas, it is important to carry a good lighting system on your helmet. There are various kinds, so take advice before buying.

Clothing must preserve body heat and prevent exposure, so, over warm underclothes, wear a roomy one-piece boiler suit or a close-fitting neoprene wet-suit. Strong boots, rubber-soled, with eyelets inset, so that they cannot catch on anything, a whistle and belay length of nylon rope. For a detailed description of equipment see *Potholing and Caving*, by Don Robinson, in the *Know the Game* series, published by E.P. Group of Companies, price 25p.

6. Gliding

How to Learn. Training. Equipment. Clothes. Books.

Gliding is very much a co-operative effort in which you are expected to help others to fly as well as flying yourself. It is this balance of friendly mucking-in together on the ground, and complete solitude and self-sufficiency in the air, that is so satisfying. Above all, gliders are the most beautiful machines ever invented and Britain is, amazingly, still a lovely country from the air.

Michael Bird, *Glider pilot, London Gliding Club*

HOW TO LEARN

The first step is to join a gliding club, of which there are at least ninety distributed over most counties of England, with at least three in Wales. You can get a list of names and addresses from the official body – The British Gliding Association, Kimberley House, Vaughan Way, Leicester. This also gives you information about each club and about holiday courses.

The subscription to your local gliding club covers the use of the club's gliders but you pay for each launch and for flying time. The subscription costs between £10 and £20 p.a. with entrance fees of from £5 to £8. Gliding is an all-year-round sport and some of the larger clubs offer holiday courses from April to September; some cater specifically for families. Children over twelve years of age are also accepted on certain courses (but no one may fly solo under the age of sixteen).

Most clubs nowadays operate from flat sites and not from the tops of hills, and rely on thermals for most of their soaring. Launching to 1000 feet is mostly done by cable, towed by a car or wound in a winch, or to 2000 feet by towing behind a light aircraft. Powered two-seater trainers which can take off under their own 'steam' are now used at a few clubs. They cut down training time to weeks instead of months, since the trainer-glider is not so dependent for take-off on the weather, but not all clubs can afford them.

TRAINING

At most clubs you will find a trained instructor who will prepare you for the tests you have to pass. After a considerable amount of instructional flying in a two-seater glider you take the *A & B* test which consists of three solo circuits of the airfield, and earns you the solo pilot's badge.

EQUIPMENT

Once you are a qualified pilot, to avoid queueing for the club gliders, it is usual to join a syndicate or form one yourself. You may meet other club members willing to accept you in a co-ownership group, or to help you form one. Or you could advertise in the specialist aeronautical press.

Gliders can cost between £900 for a second-hand single-seater and £7000 for the most modern craft. Repairs and maintenance are fairly simple and are often carried out by the group themselves. Launching will cost approximately £1·50 for a tow with a light aircraft or about 50p for a tow with a car.

CLOTHES

In winter a warm anorak, cap, gloves and slacks. Warm waterproof footwear, but not heavy boots. In summer avoid sunburn, wear good sunglasses and don't forget that the air at 2000 feet is cooler than on the ground so sunbathing gear is not recommended.

BOOKS

The British Gliding Association publish a useful booklist available on request, and four books which are helpful to the beginner: *Know the Weather*, published by the Royal Meteorological Society, 35p; *Elementary Gliding*, by P. Blanchard, 50p; *Laws and Rules for Glider Pilots*, 35p, all post free and all published by BGA. You can join the BGA for £2·20 a year and for a further £3·15 you will recieve their bi-monthly magazine *Sailplane and Gliding*.

7. Pony Trekking

How to Learn.   Where to Go.   Children Under Twelve.
Clothes.

HOW TO LEARN

Pony trekking is an easy-to-learn and pleasant pursuit
which takes you at walking pace across moors and
through woods, over hills and dales in such lovely
countryside as Dartmoor, Exmoor, the South Downs
and the Cotswolds. Only the most elementary instruction
is given in most trekking centres although some establishments employ British Horse Society assistant instructors.
Expect to be stiff the first day or two and even a bit
saddle-sore, but that soon wears off.

WHERE TO GO

There are thousands of riding centres in Britain, many of which are said to be sub-standard, so Ponies of Britain, a voluntary society, and the responsible body, have published a full descriptive list – 'Approved Trekking and Riding Holidays List', price 30p, post free, available from them at Brookside Farm, Ascot, Berkshire, which gives details of pony trekking and riding holidays, and riding courses.

Residential centres vary in their amenities. You are usually expected to share a room. Terms are usually inclusive and costs vary according to accommodation, from about £20 to £45 a week. Beware of any place charging under £20 a week for full board/accommodation – either you, or the ponies, or both, may be underfed. For the more experienced riders, a few centres provide post trekking from one centre to another.

Trekking goes on from mid-April to the end of September, but some centres in the Lake District continue into October. Most centres take one-week bookings from Saturday to Saturday inclusive and some offer two-week and weekend holidays. Treks vary in length according to the difficulty of the terrain, but generally the riding day starts at 10 am and ends about 4 pm. Centres will want to know your previous riding experience and your weight so that they can allot you a suitable mount.

CHILDREN UNDER TWELVE

For families with children over twelve, pony trekking is a fine way of getting to know large tracts of country with the added interest of having a pony to cope with. Ponies of Britain do not consider pony trekking suitable for children under twelve, who are said to get tired and bored. Riding holidays with instruction on different aspects of pony care are recommended for the younger ones where there are other children and more variety. *Activity Holidays in England*, price 60p plus 10p postage from the English Tourist Board, 4 Grosvenor Gardens, London SW1W 0DU, gives details of the kind of riding courses offered and the ages of children acceptable at the various centres in England, and the British Tourist Authority also publish a booklet, 'Pony Trekking and Riding', which covers Wales and Scotland as well: obtainable free from the BTA, 64 St James's Street, London, SW1A 1NF.

CLOTHES

You will need corduroy or whipcord trousers or, of course, jodhpurs or riding breeches (jeans are not recommended as they can cause rubbing); a waterproof anorak, or a hacking jacket or a riding mackintosh. Shoes or boots must have heels and children should always wear hard riding hats. These can sometimes be borrowed or hired from the Centre.

8. Sailing

How to Learn. Courses. Children. Equipment. Clothes.

Sailing is very much a family occupation, and when families are once hooked on it they are not likely to consider any other way of spending their time off. But it is not a sport you can take up casually after spending a weekend or two on someone's boat. There is a lot to learn, and since the ways of the sea, lake, or stretch of water which you are sailing on, are unpredictable and can be lethal, it is essential to know exactly what you are doing for the safety of yourself and your crew, and of other craft, too.

HOW TO LEARN

Whatever your age, the best way to learn to handle a
boat safely under any conditions is to take a course at a
sailing school and you will find people of all ages attend-
ing these courses. The schools are not necessarily on the
sea, there is inland sailing on lakes, lochs and reservoirs
all over the country, and more than 200 RYA recognized
teaching establishments. You can get a list of their names
and addresses, post free, from the Royal Yachting
Association (the national authority for sailing) Victoria
Way, Woking, Surrey GU21 1EQ. But the guide which
gives you full details of instruction centres and courses
is *Learn to Sail*, available from the Royal Yachting
Association, 20p, post free. From it you can choose the
Centre which best suits your particular needs.

COURSES

The cost of courses varies considerably with the centre.
Sports Council sailing centres charge about £30 a week,
while some commercially run schools might cost double,
or less or more.

At most schools running RYA courses you have a
choice of two kinds; a holiday course where you learn
the basics of handling a boat, usually a sixteen-foot
dinghy, probably of the *Wayfarer* class; you swim, sun-
bathe and have fun as well; then there are specific
courses for the National Proficiency Scheme which are
taken more seriously and for which certificates are
awarded as a result of tests.

Some holiday courses run by the Sports Council follow
the syllabus for the RYA National Elementary Day Boat
(dinghy) Certificate and students can opt to be assessed
for the certificate once they are on the course.

You can become a member of the Royal Yachting
Association for £5 a year and one of the advantages is
that RYA members can become associate members, for

two weeks, of the Island Cruising Club, Salcombe, Devon,
where the RYA run holidays. This gives you a chance to
see whether you would like to join the club. Non-members
can get a list of publications on all sailing subjects, post
free, from the Association.

CHILDREN

Courses for children generally start from about nine or
ten up to sixteen or seventeen, though there are several
that take children as young as eight or younger. Details
of courses from the RYA guide, *Learn to Sail* (see p. 40),
or from *Activity Holidays in England*, price 60p plus
10p postage, from the English Tourist Board, 4 Grosvenor
Gardens, London SW1W 0DU.

EQUIPMENT

Having taken your course and feeling confident to handle
a boat, you then look around for the club you want to
sail with. Here, *Boat World*, the sail and powercraft
yearbook, published by Sell's Publications Ltd, can help
you, as it contains a directory of all sailing clubs in the
British Isles, with a detailed description of every one,
including name, address, telephone number, secretary,
subscription and temporary subscription terms, boat-
yard facilities, slipways, moorings, in fact, everything
you want to know. So you can look up the area you prefer
and find out what goes on there. *Boat World* is available
in public libraries, or from Sell's Publications Ltd, Sell's
House, 39 East Street, Epsom, Surrey, price £2·35.

When you have decided on your club and have seen
what boats they sail, you may want to buy or build a
boat of your own.

The alternative to buying or building a boat is to join
a club that owns boats. There are not many of them
open to all, since most of them belong to large organizations like the Banks and the BBC and have a closed
membership.

The Island Cruising Club, the Island, Salcombe, Devon, is the exception. You can join the club for £8 a year and sail the club boats at a cost of from £20 to £45 a week according to size and season. They have thirty-seven dinghies and six cruising boats, from an eighty-ton Brixham trawler to a five-berth thirty-footer. Accommodation for dinghy sailors is in the houseboats in the estuary. The larger boats carry staff-member skippers who are in command of the boats.

CLOTHES

The first essential is a life-jacket – there are several types to choose from – which should be worn at all times on the boat however good a swimmer you are.

It is always colder afloat than ashore so you will need some or all of the following: two thick jerseys, jeans, neck towel, waterproof smock and trousers (held up by braces), waterproof hat, socks, 'sailing' shoes with special honeycombed soles available from sailing shops. If it is really cold, wet-suits (sleeveless) are useful, but as they are slippery and are apt to tear you should wear clothes over them. It is a good idea to keep spare clothes in a waterproof bag.

9. Underwater Swimming: Snorkelling and Aqualung Diving

How to Learn.   Snorkelling for Children.   Equipment.
Where to Swim.   Holiday Courses.

I think the main appeal of underwater swimming is that you enter a totally different environment and what you see is completely new. Although you are always with others, you are very much alone too – the enjoyment and experience is very personal. There is something special about weightlessness in that you can remain motionless and become part of the environment along with its native inhabitants. You take on an extra dimension yourself.
Jill Sarsby, *London Branch, British Sub-Aqua Club*

HOW TO LEARN

Underwater swimming is an 'adventure' sport and because it takes place in an alien environment, the strictest safety measures must be observed. The best way to find out about them and to get safe training, is to join the British Sub-Aqua Club, the governing body of the sport, 70 Brompton Road, London SW3 1HA, which has 600 branches throughout the world, mostly in large towns. BSAC has strict safety standards and tests which must be passed before any member can begin to use an aqualung. Members under fifteen are not encouraged to use an aqualung, but it is a good idea for them to learn to snorkel in a swimming pool.

The entrance fee to BSAC is £3 and the subscription is £4·58 p.a. plus any levy the local branch may charge. If you are a member of the BSAC you may dive with other branches if you are in their area, subject, naturally, to their permission.

SNORKELLING FOR CHILDREN

The National Snorkellers' Club – the children's section of the BSAC – is open to all children throughout the country from the age of nine to seventeen who can swim competently. Through the club, which has branches all over Britain, you can learn in a swimming pool how to use mask, fins, and snorkel, safely. This costs you a nominal entrance charge and about 10p a time for the use of the baths which the club has booked specially.

The club runs a Snorkellers' Award Scheme, which consists of proficiency tests open to children from nine upwards. When you have passed these you rate as a 'Snorkel Diver'. From there you can progress to snorkelling in the sea, where you can inspect the strange wild life of the sea bed and after that, when you are fifteen, you can go on to aqualung diving.

All information is available from the Director of the

National Snorkellers' Club, 13 Langham Gardens, Wembley, Middlesex HA0 3RG. The information includes a full list of clubs and instructors. Branches charge a small entrance fee to cover the cost of the log-book in which the menber keeps the full record of his achievement.

EQUIPMENT

For *snorkelling* you need mask, fins and snorkel. For *aqualung diving* you need in addition a cylinder (from £40), a demand valve (between £30 and £60), a harness (£10), a wet-suit (readymade about £35–£60; in kit form about £22), a weight belt (£2–£4) and a watch (from £30 upwards). A mask costs between £3 and £10, fins £2·50 to £10·00 and a snorkel tube about £1. Beginners may usually hire equipment from their branch for a modest fee. At some clubs you can get good second-hand equipment or you may get a discount off new equipment bought through the club.

Mask. Wear a mask that covers the eyes and the nose and has a window of toughened glass and a 'compensator' so that you can grip your nose. *Never* wear goggles or a full face mask that covers the mouth or a mask with a built-in snorkel tube.

Fins. These should be full fitting and comfortable, not too loose to chafe, or too tight to cause cramp.

Aqualung Cylinder. This contains the compressed air which enables the diver to remain underwater. It has to be maintained very carefully to avoid possible accidents.

Demand Valve. This adjusts the flow of air so that the diver breathes in the correct amount at the right pressure. *Never* wear ear plugs or nose clips.

Once a diver has been diving regularly and is proficient,

he or she can begin to specialize – in underwater photography, marine biology, the study of wrecks, even collecting antiques (ancient bottles etc.) off the sea bed. Many of these subjects are covered by the clubs.

Full details of techniques are contained in the BSAC *Diving Manual*, which each member receives free when he joins. It is also available at public libraries. For preliminary information on snorkelling see the BSAC *Snorkelling Manual*, available from the BSAC Bookshop, 38 Oxford Street, Whitstable, Kent, price 80p, post free.

WHERE TO SWIM

The most interesting, and therefore the most popular areas for underwater swimming, are the coasts of Dorset, Devon and Cornwall, the Scilly Isles, Pembrokeshire, Anglesey, the Lleyn peninsula and the Northumbrian coast, in particular the Farne Islands. All round the Scottish coast is good if you avoid the main industrial areas.

HOLIDAY COURSES

Aqualung Diving. The Fort Bovisand Underwater Centre runs a two-week training course every month from May to October which leads to the British Sub-Aqua Club third-class grade of proficiency. It is open to competent swimmers over fifteen. All-inclusive fee is £70. Details from them at above address.

Two, one-week introductory courses are held in early August by the South Western Sports Council at Wareham, Dorset. These introduce you to the sport and show you how to use the aqualung equipment. You live under canvas and the all-inclusive fee for one week is £25. Open to competent swimmers over fifteen. Details from the British Sub-Aqua Club, address p. 44.

Snorkelling. The National Snorkellers' Club runs two

holiday courses: twelve days in Majorca or Southern Spain at Whitsun, for children aged eleven to seventeen, whether members or not. The course costs about £60, which includes air travel as well as full board and lodging in a hotel. The party consists of fifty children and a staff of ten, including two trained nurses.

During August the club runs a summer camping holiday for boys only. Those who go must hold the Snorkellers' Award, i.e. they must have passed the necessary tests (see p. 44). The course is held in the Channel Islands, the Isle of Man or some similar island. Twelve days costs about £30, inclusive of board, lodging and travel. The party consists of forty, plus a full staff.

On all holiday courses snorkellers take their own masks, fins and snorkels.

For further details of snorkelling clubs or courses write to Lionel Blandford, Director of the BSAC National Snorkellers' Club, 13 Langham Gardens, Wembley, Middlesex HA0 3RG.

10. Walking

What to Wear. Plan your Route.

Walking is not something you 'take up' as you take up golf or sailing – after all, it does 'come naturally' – but if you take to tramping long distances in remote country-side or on hills you should be properly equipped against the weather and prepared for emergencies, which can mean anything from getting lost in a thick mist, to being immobilized as a result of a sprained ankle. In fact, unless you are wearing the right clothes you will not enjoy the lovely long treks over the moors – you will be more concerned with blistered feet, wet clothes, nettle stings and scratches.

The following recommendations come largely from the
Ramblers' Association, 1–4 Crawford Mews, York Street,
London W1H 1PT, who are the authority on everything
to do with walking. You can join the Association for £2
a year with concessionary rates for married couples,
retired people, students and young people. This is what
they say about equipment.

Feet. The experienced walker will wear boots with uppers
of leather and moulded rubber soles – 'Vibram' or
'Commando' are recommended. With them he will wear
two pairs of socks, a thin pair next to the skin and a
thicker pair over them. Sandals or plimsolls are unsuitable since they give you no support or protection. If you
are reluctant to spend money on boots, for what may be
only an occasional holiday, then wear strong shoes with
uppers of leather and rubber moulded soles as described
above.

Clothes.   They should be comfortable, warm and windproof. Thin, cotton jeans are not suitable for long walks.
Trousers should be of strong material and worn with a
comfortable shirt, and a wind-and-waterproof anorak
with a hood. This is all that you need in summer. In
winter, add a woollen jumper and for very cold weather,
two medium-weight jumpers – better than one thick one
– warm gloves or mittens and a close-fitting beret. The
anorak should cover the trunk and should be completely
windproof.

On long-distance walks you should regard *four as a
minimum* in any party, particularly on the hills. Should
there be an accident one can stay with the casualty while
the other two go for help.

PLAN YOUR ROUTE

An Ordnance Survey map of 1″, 1/50000, or 2½″ scale is

the first essential in planning a walk. (The 1″ Ordnance Survey map is gradually being replaced by the 1/50000.) Allow yourself plenty of time to get to your destination before it gets dark. Reckon to do 2 mph plus another hour for every 1500 feet climbed. As well as a map, carry a compass (of the 'Silva' type) a watch and a whistle. Take a small frameless rucksack to carry food, a waterproof cape and an extra pair of socks.

Keep an eye on the *weather* and don't rely entirely on forecasts. Mountain weather changes rapidly and mists can envelop you in a few minutes.

Before setting out, say where you are going and when, approximately, you expect to be back.

11. Water Skiing

How to Learn.   Equipment.   Holiday Courses.

Water skiing is essentially a sport for the whole family, whatever age they may be. Seventy-year-olds have been known to take it up and children start as soon as they can swim.

It is surprisingly easy to learn and most skiers are self-taught, but you must be able to swim at least fifty yards, and you are advised to wear a life-jacket at all times. You will get pure enjoyment out of skimming the surface at about 25 mph and a wonderful sense of speed and daring, even if you never get to the slalom and jump stage. And if you can face the cold, you can ski all the year round.

The best way to start is to join a club, of which there are over one hundred affiliated to the British Water Ski Federation, 70 Brompton Road, London, SW3 1EG. The Federation will send you a list of names and addresses on request. Most clubs offer boat and driver facilities and most have clubhouses, ranging from the spartan to the luxurious. Membership fees vary accordingly but the average is about £10 to £20 a year, and the cost of a seven- or eight-minute ski run is from 50p to about £2 including the hire of skis. While you are learning you can usually borrow or hire equipment from the club, but when you are no longer a beginner you will have to buy your own. Not all clubs hire out equipment, even temporarily.

EQUIPMENT

You will need:

Skis.   It is a good idea to try out various kinds of skis at your club before you decide on what to buy, as there are variations of material, size and shape. Choose skis to suit your purpose, your weight and the speed of the towing boat. A good pair of standard skis costs about £27, or you can buy a do-it-yourself kit for very much less.

Wet-suit.   In this climate you need a rubberized wet-suit. This costs from £30 upwards, or you can make it yourself from a kit for about £18.

Boat.   About 50 per cent of club members own a boat. The others use club facilities. An inflatable boat (Avon, Seacraft or Zodiac) costs about £400 and a 20 hp outboard motor (Evinrude, Mercury or Johnson are all reliable makes) costs a further £400.

HOLIDAY COURSES

At Storrs Hall Hotel, Windermere, Cumbria, the Sports Council arranges a series of one-week water skiing courses from June to September for beginners, ages seventeen to fifty, for small groups and individuals, with training from qualified instructors. The price includes the provision of all equipment. At the National Water Sports Centre at Holme Pierrepont, Nottingham NG12 2LU, there are mid-week (Monday–Friday) water skiing courses for beginners to advanced, from June to September, age nine plus; individuals and groups up to six.

Part II. Where to do What

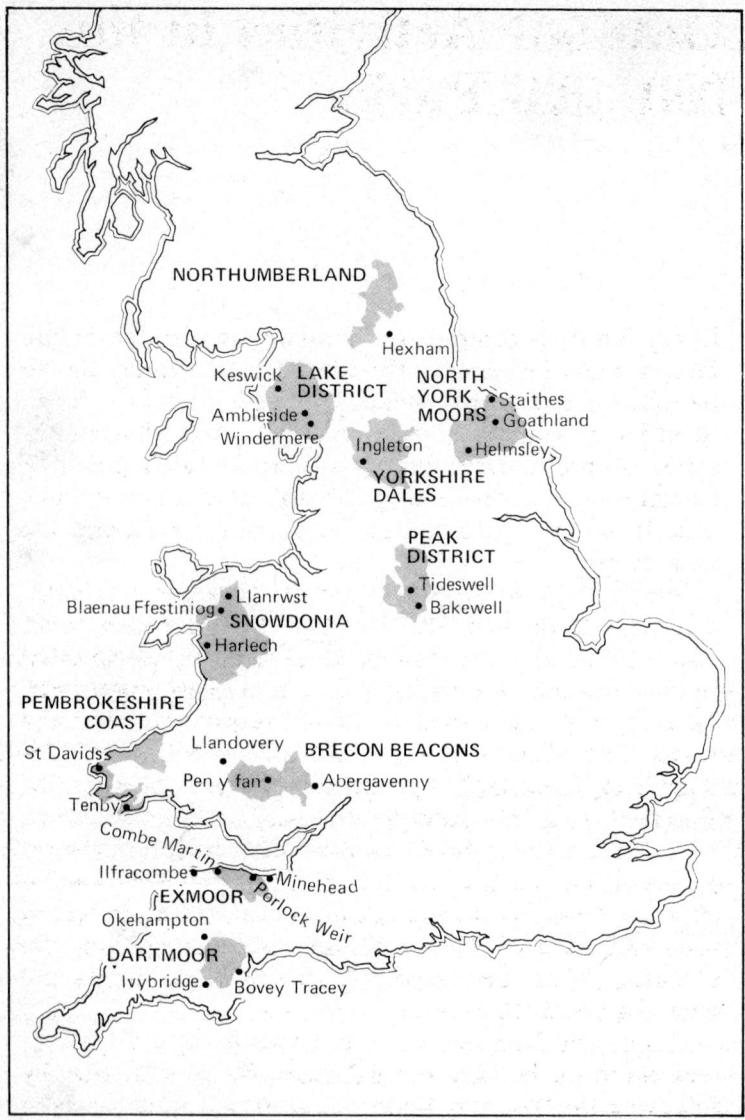

NORTHUMBERLAND

• Hexham

Keswick **LAKE**
• **DISTRICT**

**NORTH
YORK
MOORS** • Staithes
• Goathland

Ambleside •

Windermere •

Ingleton • • Helmsley

• **YORKSHIRE
DALES**

**PEAK
DISTRICT**

• Tideswell
• Bakewell

• Llanrwst

Blaenau Ffestiniog •

SNOWDONIA

• Harlech

**PEMBROKESHIRE
COAST**

St Davids

Llandovery **BRECON BEACONS**

Pen y fan • • Abergavenny

Tenby •

Combe Martin

Ilfracombe • • Minehead

EXMOOR Porlock Weir

Okehampton

DARTMOOR

Ivybridge • • Bovey Tracey

Outdoor Activities in the National Parks

Every family is composed of individuals with individual interests and hobbies, so the ideal family holiday has to be taken in a place with many different kinds of activity in order to satisfy everyone. This section describes a series of particularly interesting and varied tracts of countryside and the holiday pursuits that go on in each one. It is then up to you to decide which area best fits your family.

Facilities for holiday activities are most conveniently available in the so-called National Parks, which cover 5258 square miles of country. These are areas designated by the Countryside Commission as being specially beautiful open country suitable for holiday pursuits, and the Local Authorities have the job of 'safeguarding the landscape and ensuring that people can get there to enjoy it'. The Parks are not nationally owned, but rights of access have been agreed with landowners. There are approved paths which are kept clear, camping and caravanning sites, and centres where you can get local information on the various activities available, from potholing to canoeing. There are usually Youth Hostels, hotels and guest houses in the area.

People still live and work and own land in the Parks and those on holiday are asked to fit in with this by following the 'Country Code', i.e. shutting gates, keeping dogs under control, protecting plants and wildlife and safeguarding against all risk of fire – in fact, they are asked to respect the life of the countryside.

1. Walking the Long-Distance Footpaths

Where to Stay. The Pennine Way. The Cleveland Way. Cornwall Coast Path. The South Downs Way. Offa's Dyke Path. Pembrokeshire Coast Path. North Downs Way. The Ridgeway. Pony Trekking, Riding and Cycling.

These paths are, to quote the official wording, 'national routes with continuous rights of way offering opportunities for walkers, horse riders or cyclists to make extensive journeys that mostly avoid roads used by motor traffic'. Twelve paths have been planned; seven are open for their entire length, though you may find an occasional temporary diversion, while many others are accessible for part of the way.

There are two ways of treating long-distance paths. Either you take a whole fortnight's holiday and cover the route from start to finish or, more rewarding perhaps for a family with children between eight and fourteen, is to stay at one centre and cover different sections of the way on foot every day, coming home to roost comfortably each night.

The guide books on the whole are very good indeed especially the two published by HM Stationery Office, 49 High Holborn, London WC1V 6HB (three more are in production). Detailed maps accompany each walk and the names and addresses of Youth Hostels are included, as well as sources of other information.

WHERE TO STAY

On the long-distance path, accommodation is generally in farmhouses, cottages, guest houses and pubs, apart from Youth Hostels, and it is advisable to book ahead by telephone on the day. Only members may use Youth Hostels, but it is worthwhile joining and the membership fee is modest (54p for ages five to fifteen, £1·08 for sixteen to twenty, £1·62 for over twenty-one). It is advisable always to check in the handbook whether the hostels are open. For postal application for membership write to Youth Hostels Association, Trevelyan House, St Albans, Hertfordshire AL1 2DY. For personal application and sales, 24 John Adam Street, London WC2N 6JE.

THE PENNINE WAY

Opened in 1965, probably the most arduous of all the routes, running for 250 miles from Edale in the Peak National Park over plateaux and mountains between 2000 and 3000 feet high including Kinder Scout. The Way is often really tough going, but it is possible to choose which part you want to explore, because the landscape is infinitely varied, from gentle pasture lands in the Dales to rugged mountain country.

Further Reference. The Pennine Way by Tom Stephenson. *Long-Distance Footpath Guide No. 1,* HMSO 1969, price £1·50. Leaflet, 'The Pennine Way', free from Countryside Commission, John Dower House, Crescent Place, Cheltenham, Gloucestershire GL50 3RA.

THE CLEVELAND WAY

Opened in 1969, the Way runs for ninety-three miles through North Yorkshire and Cleveland, over the moors and along the rocky cliffs of the north-east coast with its fantastic and uplifting seascape. The route starts at Helmsley, goes north by Rievaulx Abbey to the coast at Saltburn; from there along the cliff-tops by Staithes, past Whitby and Robin Hood's Bay, to end near Filey. But beware the 'roak' – a local fog – and the eccentric habits of the Cleveland weather.

Further Reference. The Cleveland Way by Alan Falconer. *Long-Distance Footpath Guide No. 2,* HMSO 1972, price £1·80. Leaflet, 'The Cleveland Way', free from Countryside Commission (address above).

CORNWALL COAST PATH

Opened in May 1973, the path starts at Marsland Mouth in North Cornwall and, keeping as close to the coastline as possible, runs for 268 miles past all those familiar Cornish places whose names evoke an image of sun and sea: Bude, Port Isaac, Polzeath, St Ives to Land's End. Then along the south coast by Penzance, the Lizard, Polperro to Cremyll, and all villages in between. Walking from north to south you see the two faces of Cornwall. The dark cliffs of the north coast overlooking the wide, and often gale-swept Atlantic, have a stern and rugged character in contrast with the mild intimacy of the channel shore with its sheltered coves, palm trees and gentle breezes.

guide to walks of all lengths with map and Ramblers'
Accommodation Register; from County Hall, Truro,
Cornwall, 20p, plus postage. Leaflet, 'Cornwall Coast
Path', free from Countryside Commission (address p. 60).

THE SOUTH DOWNS WAY

Opened in 1972, it runs from Eastbourne, west across
Sussex to Buriton in Hampshire.

The Way, which starts at Beachy Head (an alternative
route begins outside Eastbourne), follows the line of the
Downs above the coast, touching at such favourite places
as Alfriston, Ditchling Beacon, 813 feet above sea level
and the highest point of the Downs, where the view all
round is superb; across the Arun river at Houghton,
when the landscape suddenly changes from open rolling
turf to wooded country and forests; to Bignor, where you
can see what is said to be the largest Roman villa in
Britain, through pine forest to Cocking Down and Linch
Down and so to the Hartings and Hampshire.

The Way is ideal for single-day walks or weekend
outings, since you can usually leave your car at a nearby
town or village, or you can go by bus and be independent.
There are several Youth Hostels near the Way, and
pubs, guest houses and hotels, so accommodation is not
a great problem. For those who prefer riding to walking,
the South Downs Way is the first long-distance approved
bridleway. For details of stabling and routes see the section 'Pony Trekking, Riding, and Cycling', at the end
of this chapter.

Further Reference. Leaflet, 'The South Downs Way',
free from Countryside Commission (address p. 60).

OFFA'S DYKE PATH

Opened in 1971, it runs for 168 miles from Prestatyn in
the north to Sedbury Cliffs near Chepstow on the Severn

estuary in the south. The path coincides for sixty miles of its length with the original Offa's Dyke built in AD 785 by Offa, King of Mercia, to mark the boundary between the English and the Welsh. The toughest going of all the approved paths except for parts of the Pennine Way. Its historic associations, archaeological sites, its really magnificent views and castles, on and off the route, make the Path well worth attempting, in sections at least. Essential to be adequately clothed and shod and equipped with maps and guide books.

Further Reference. The Offa's Dyke Path by Arthur Roberts, a detailed guide from south to north, published by Ramblers' Association, 1–4 Crawford Mews, London W1H 1PT, price 15p, plus postage. Leaflet, 'Offa's Dyke', free from Countryside Commission (address p. 60).

PEMBROKESHIRE COAST PATH

From St Dogmaels in the north to Amroth in the south. Most of the way on cliff-top, past great headlands, splendidly remote. Seabirds and seals. Interesting geology. Magnificent views. 170 miles.

NORTH DOWNS WAY

From Farnham to Dover, through two designated Areas of Outstanding Natural Beauty – the Surrey Hills and Kent Downs. At the moment only forty-three miles from Hollingbourne to Dover are open. 141 miles.

THE RIDGEWAY

From Overton Hill near Avebury in Wiltshire, to Ivinghoe Beacon in Buckinghamshire, taking in the North Wessex Downs and the Chilterns, both designated Areas of Outstanding Natural Beauty. 85 miles.

The only long-distance bridleway open to horse riders and cyclists is the South Downs Way. You can get a leaflet with information on stabling and grazing en route, from Charles Shippam, Priory Cottage, Box Grove, Chichester, West Sussex, in return for a stamped addressed envelope. Horses to hire are not available locally for the whole length of the Way, only for sections of it. So if you intend riding the entire length, either you take your own, or borrow.

There are also forty miles of the Ridgeway going westwards from Goring to Avebury which are available to riders and cyclists. On most of the long-distance footpaths you will find stretches open to riders and cyclists. Local Information Centres should be able to give you help on this.

Incidentally, a bridleway that is open to horse riders, is automatically open to cyclists as well, and vice versa.

2. Brecon Beacons

*Walking. Pony Trekking. Angling. Boating,
Canoeing and Canal Cruising. Caving. Geology.
Archaeology. Accommodation. Camping and
Caravanning. Information Centres. Day Outings and
Weekends. Further Reference.*

This National Park is made up of 519 square miles of
moors, forest, green valleys with sparkling, rushing
rivers and waterfalls, acres of common grazing, and
dominated by the great range of the Black Mountains
extending from Carmarthenshire (Dyfed) in the west
to Monmouthshire (Gwent) in the east. In the middle are
the Brecon Beacons which rise to 2907 feet in Pen y Fan.

The Park is a countryside of contrasts, with rounded hills
and steep mountainsides. The limestone area produces
fantastic caves and through the Park run thirty-two
miles of the Brecon to Newport canal, lovely to cruise on
and to walk beside.

If you want to birdwatch, fish for trout or salmon, go
caving, pony trekking, boating, or just walk for miles and
look at a few ruined castles or prehistoric monuments,
then you can do it all in the Park.

WALKING

Obviously this is superb country for walking of all kinds,
whether you choose hill walking along the ridge routes
of the Black Mountains, or scrambling to the top of Pen
y Fan. You can walk along the wooded valleys or through
the Great Forest where there is much to entice the
geologist and the naturalist. Or follow the routes that
take you from one Youth Hostel to another – there are
six Youth Hostels in or near the Park. Or climb to
the Mountain Centre, 1100 feet up on the high moor of
Mynydd Illtud, where you can rest, picnic or have a
meal. You can even join in field study work using the
Centre as a base. (See leaflet on the Mountain Centre,
available from the Supervisor, the Mountain Centre,
Libanus, near Brecon, Powys.)

PONY TREKKING

Pony trekking or hacking are two of the best ways of
seeing the country, and the Black Mountain routes and
the Beacons provide good riding country. There are over
twenty stables in the area, most of which offer accommodation usually in guest houses, farmhouses or hotels,
or camping for those who prefer it. Some stables undertake trail riding, a round trip with overnight stops at
different places. For names, addresses and prices see
leaflet, 'Pony Trekking', from Information Centres
(see end of chapter).

Good, particularly for trout and salmon; some coarse fishing. Much of the water is privately owned, but day or season tickets are often available. Rod licences and permits from owners of fishing rights are essential.

Trout and Salmon Fishing.   On rivers Wye and Usk; in rivers Hepste, Mellte, Nedd and Pyrddin, where there are also sea trout, and in the river Towy and tributaries – sea trout also. Most water is private but tickets can be had for specific stretches.

You can also fish for trout in more than six different reservoirs where day tickets are available, some considerably more expensive than others.

Coarse Fishing.   In the river Wye for pike, dace, perch, roach etc., and in Llangorse Lake – permits are necessary, see below.

A leaflet 'Fishing' gives details of where to fish for what, plus addresses of where to get licences and permits. It can be got from Information Centres (see end of chapter).

BOATING, CANOEING AND CANAL CRUISING

Where so much of the rivers is given over to fishing it is not always easy to accommodate those interested in boats, but there are limited stretches of the Usk and the Wye open to the canoeist and rower and there is canal cruising and pleasure boating on the Monmouthshire and Brecon Canal. You can also take boat trips on the rivers and a 'canal bus' operates all year. Further details can be found in *Boating and Sailing*, from Information Centres (see end of chapter).

CAVING

This is caving country and has some of the deepest

and longest caves in Britain. At least seven caving clubs
operate in the area and they are usually prepared to help
experienced cavers but cannot undertake beginners.
Club houses are normally open to visiting cavers by
previous arrangement with the club secretary.

For a detailed list of caves and clubs see 'Caving',
available from Information Centres. (Show caves at
Dan-yr-Ogof in the Tawe Valley are open daily.)

GEOLOGY

The Park is of great interest to geologists and geological
exhibits are on view in the Brecknock Museum, Glamorgan Street, Brecon.

ARCHAEOLOGY

For archaeologists there are prehistoric hill forts to visit,
barrows and standing stones, including the largest Iron
Age fort in Wales – Garn Goch. Near Brecon there is Y
Gaer, a Roman fort excavated by Sir Mortimer Wheeler.
There are some fine bridges and ruined castles.

ACCOMMODATION

Hotels in the towns, otherwise guest houses and farmhouses. Some furnished cottages to rent. Leaflet from
Information Centres. The Ramblers' Association produce
a Register of bed-and-breakfast accommodation covering
the whole country, which you can get from them at 1–4
Crawford Mews, London W1H 1PT, for 30p plus 8p
postage.

CAMPING AND CARAVANNING

There are a number of approved sites not far from towns,
with varying facilities, in Breconshire (Powys), Carmar-

thenshire (Dyfed), and Monmouthshire (Gwent) and certain sites for members of the Caravan Club. A list with full details of facilities and prices, names and addresses is available from Information Centres.

INFORMATION CENTRES

Abergavenny – Lower Monk Street; Libanus – Mountain Centre; Llandovery – 8 Broad Street. Written enquiries to 6 Glamorgan Street, Brecon LD3 7DW.

DAY OUTINGS AND WEEKENDS

For day outings by road the National Park (at Brecon) is within easy reach of: Cardiff, 42 miles; Swansea, 39; Hereford, 36; Gloucester, 60. For weekends, from Brecon by road, Birmingham is only 84 miles; Coventry, 102; Stoke, 112; Manchester, 114, and London 164.

FURTHER REFERENCE

Brecon Beacons National Park Guide, available from HM Stationery Office, 49 High Holborn, London WC1V 6HB, or from Information Centre, 6 Glamorgan Street, Brecon LD3 7DW, price 50p.

3. Dartmoor

Walking. Pony Trekking. Geology. Archaeology.
Angling. Wild Life. Places to Visit. Accommodation.
Camping and Caravanning. Information Centres.
Day Outings and Weekends. Books.

The National Park is 365 square miles of moorland and rounded hills, of rivers and valleys, right in the middle of Devon. It stretches from Okehampton in the north, to Ivybridge in the south, and from Tavistock in the west, to Bovey Tracey in the east. Most of the Park is a plateau from 1000 to 1500 feet high, the hills rising to over 2000 feet. It is a land of streams and rivers; twelve of Devon's rivers rise in Dartmoor.

The wide landscape is punctuated by charming little villages, with ancient churches and farmhouses, granite crosses and a wealth of prehistoric monuments.

Being high and hilly, the climate is cool, 5°F. less than on the Devon coast, and the rainfall is heavy, though the eastern end of the Park is drier than the west. Fog and mist are fairly common and can come down suddenly but the weather changes quickly and the Moor on a bright sunny day with a fresh wind blowing is unbeatable.

WALKING

Dartmoor is primarily walking and riding country, with a tradition of access over any land which is predominantly moor or common, so that you can wander on the moor for miles and for days without hindrance.

Leaflets describing all sorts of short walks can be got from Information Centres (see end of chapter). For longer walks consult the official guide to the National Park (see end of chapter). Besides the splendid landscape there are stone circles, 'clapper' bridges and prehistoric settlements to be seen.

Beware, though, of the intruding Ministry of Defence, who have a huge tract of land from Okehampton to Great Mis Tor for artillery practice and a rifle range at Rippon Tor. This is an area you should avoid during practice, the dates and times of which can be got from local post offices. Red flags are always flown during firing.

Long-distance walkers should be properly equipped with strong shoes or boots and waterproof clothing and in view of the likelihood of mist or fog, it is not a bad idea to take a compass.

PONY TREKKING

Probably the best way to explore Dartmoor is on the back of a pony. There are a large number of riding stables

and you can get a list of names, addresses and telephone
numbers from Information Centres (see end of chapter).

GEOLOGY

The geological feature which dominates the area is
Dartmoor granite, of which the greater part of the
National Park is formed, but there are other rocks of
interest around the Park which intrigue geologists and
there is an interesting chapter on the subject by Dr
Alfred Shorter in the official guide.

ARCHAEOLOGY

For archaeologists the Park is rich in prehistoric relics,
Megalithic tombs, Bronze Age stone rows, cairns and
cists. There are relics too of the twelfth century 'tin
rush' and you can still see the remains of blowing-houses
where the tin ore was smelted. A leaflet, 'Antiquities', is
available free from Information Centres (see end of
chapter).

ANGLING

Fly fishing only, for salmon, sea trout and brown trout.
All the rivers are privately owned, but it is possible to get
permits – season, weekly or daily – to fish the water that
belongs to the Duchy of Cornwall, that is, most of the
East Dart river and the West Dart as far as Dartmeet
and some smaller tributaries. (Rod permits are also
necessary.) Otherwise permission to fish elsewhere must
be sought from the owner of the fishing rights. Details of
licences, permits etc., in a leaflet entitled 'Fly Fishing',
from Information Centres (see end of chapter).

WILD LIFE

Foxes, badgers and otters are native to the area but are

rarely seen. Mink have escaped and become established in the river banks. In the water they look like small otters.

Birds.   On the moors and high places there are buzzards, ravens, kestrels, and in the wooded valleys, chaffinches, nuthatches, marsh tits and green woodpeckers. You may also see on the moors, skylarks, meadow pipits and red grouse, and among rocks, wheatears, and by the rivers, dippers and grey wagtails.

Butterflies.   In the height of summer you may see Large Whites, Small Tortoiseshells, Painted Ladies and Red Admirals; the Emperor moth and the Fox moth. Round the streams you may see dragonflies.

PLACES TO VISIT

Buckfast Abbey, rebuilt on a medieval foundation. Buckland in the Moor, a typical Devon village with thatched moorstone cottages. Brentor, a volcanic cone on the western edge of the Park. Dartmeet, a combination of moor and valley landscape. For other places of special interest, see the official guide to the National Park (see end of chapter).

ACCOMMODATION

For a list of hotels and guest houses, write to South Dartmoor Tourist Association, Leusdon Lodge, Townsgate, Ashburton, Devon, or consult the Ramblers' Association Register, see p. 67.

CAMPING AND CARAVANNING

There are a considerable number of caravan parks and camping sites in and around Dartmoor National Park, all of which are listed in the booklet, 'Devon Camping

Sites for Tents and Touring Caravans', available from Information Centres and by post from Devon County Council Planning Department, County Hall, Exeter, on receipt of a stamped addressed envelope, 9" × 6". No camping is allowed in the Park without permission from the landowner and this includes moorland. Campers are, therefore, encouraged to use the recognized sites. There are seven Youth Hostels in or near the Park. Details from Information Centres or from the Youth Hostels Association (address on p. 59).

INFORMATION CENTRES

At Ashburton, Bovey Tracey, Buckfastleigh, Moreton-hampstead, Newton Abbot, Okehampton, Plymouth, Tavistock, Two Bridges. Written enquiries to County Hall, Exeter.

DAY OUTINGS AND WEEKENDS

For day outings the Dartmoor National Park is within easy reach by road of most of Devon and much of Cornwall. For weekends, Bristol and Bath are only about 118 miles from Tavistock; Cardiff 161 and London 204 miles.

BOOKS

Dartmoor National Park, Guide No. 1, price 44p, published by HM Stationery Office, 49 High Holborn, London WC1V 6HB. Written orders to HMSO, PO Box 569, London SE1 9NH. A comprehensive list entitled 'Publications on Devon and the Dartmoor and Exmoor National Parks', is available free from the Information Centre, County Hall, Exeter.

4. Exmoor

Walking. Riding. Angling. Archaeology. Geology.
Wild Life. Sailing. Swimming. Accommodation.
Camping and Caravanning. Information Centres. Day
Outings and Weekends. Further Reference.

Exmoor consists of 265 square miles of National Park mostly in Somerset but extending into Devon. It reaches from near Minehead in the east to near Ilfracombe in the west. Its north coast has particularly dramatic cliffs and steep gorges with rivers rushing to the sea. Inland is heathery moor, bare grass hills and the high plateau of Dunkery Beacon, 1704 feet up, ideal for walking and riding.

WALKING

The whole area is perfect walking country apart from the bogs on the moors, and these are not dangerous. Access is available almost everywhere and paths are way-marked. Booklets on way-marked walks are available from Minehead Information Centre (see end of chapter).

A long-distance footpath, thirty-two miles of it, crosses the Park giving magnificent seascapes to the Welsh coast opposite. A night's accommodation can usually be found in farms or cottages except at the height of the season, when you must book well in advance.

RIDING

Next to walking, riding is the best way to explore Exmoor and there are stables for all kinds of riding, from an hour's hacking to days of pony trekking. You can get a fully detailed list of riding establishments from the Information Centres (see end of chapter).

ANGLING

Any amount of sporting fishing, mostly dry fly, in rivers and streams, for little brown trout usually about eight to ten inches long. Not many deep pools. Some stretches of water available for public fishing, otherwise rod and line licences are essential, as is permission from the owner of the fishing rights. Salmon fishing in the lower reaches of the Exe and Barle. A free leaflet, 'River and Freshwater Fishing', gives details of stretches, owners etc., and hotels with fishing rights, available from Information Centres (see end of chapter).

Sea Fishing. Good. From boats with rod or line at Porlock Weir, Combe Martin and Minehead, or off rocks or from the harbour. Skate, conger, bass and whiting on the rod. Mackerel, pollack and bass on line. For heavier fish, further out to sea, you can hire a motor boat and take a party. Apply to the relevant harbour master. A free leaflet, 'Fishing Hints', describes the best spots to fish, obtainable from Information Centres.

ARCHAEOLOGY

There is a vast amount of archaeological interest in Exmoor including stone circles, standing stones and two Roman signal stations. Enough at least to occupy an aspiring archaeologist for a fortnight. See the leaflet, 'The Archaeology of the Exmoor District', from Information Centres.

GEOLOGY

The district is specially interesting because of its rock

structure. For the layman, unusual rock exposures are to be seen in old quarries and a fine 'storm beach' at Porlock Bay.

WILD LIFE

The only wild red deer in England in large herds are to be seen on Exmoor, that is, if you can manage to catch a glimpse of them.

Birdwatching. Owing to the variety of scenery this is a particularly good area for birdwatching. Ravens, buzzards, occasional harriers and very rarely, kites, on the moors, and many freshwater, woodland and sea birds.

SAILING

There is sailing at Minehead, Porlock Weir and Ilfracombe, which have beautiful harbours but also problems of drying out at low water. Minehead Sailing Club accepts temporary members.

SWIMMING

Wide sands for bathing at Minehead, and incidentally you can launch a dinghy off them. Most of the coves along the coast are safe for bathing, but swimming off headlands, including Warren, and in certain bays outside the Park area can be very dangerous.

ACCOMMODATION

Six Youth Hostels in the area and good farm and guest house accommodation as well as hotels. Free leaflets on all the subjects mentioned above, except Sailing, can be had from Exmoor National Park Information Centre at Minehead (address at end of chapter) which is open all year. For Youth Hostel information write to the Youth Hostels Association, address on p. 59.

There are caravan and tent sites all over the area and in particular at Ilfracombe, Barnstaple, Minehead, Watchet and Porlock. Detailed descriptions of sites are available in a free leaflet from Information Centres.

INFORMATION CENTRES

Combe Martin, The Beach Car Park; Lynton, Lyn and Exmoor Museum, Market Street; written enquiries to Exmoor National Park Information Centre, Market House, The Parade, Minehead, Somerset.

DAY OUTINGS AND WEEKENDS

Exmoor National Park and the surrounding countryside is an ideal area for day outings or weekends from Exeter, Bristol and Bath, which are all under eighty miles away by car, from, say, Minehead. London is only 169 miles by road. Long-distance motor coaches run to Taunton, Barnstaple, Ilfracombe and Minehead from most regional centres.

FURTHER REFERENCE

HMSO, *Guide Book to Exmoor*, edited by J. Coleman-Cooke, price 42½p; 'Bibliography', a leaflet listing recommended books, is available free. Both available from the Information Centre at Minehead.

5. Lake District National Park

*Walking. Fell Walking. Climbing. Pony Trekking
and Riding. Sailing. Canoeing. Boating.
Water Skiing. Birdwatching. Angling. Gliding.
Archaeology. Accommodation. Information Centres.
Access.*

The Park's 866 square miles of fells and valleys include
sixteen lakes, at least twenty mountain passes and eleven
groups of mountain peaks. Such statistics make the Lake
District seem enormous and fearsome, but all these
splendours are compactly contained within the Park

which is not much more than forty miles across. You don't have to walk for miles over the great, open spaces before you reach a landmark of some kind. It is this contrast between the gentle, wooded valleys and the steep, stark, craggy mountains, that gives the Lake District its peculiar charm.

The Lakes themselves are different in size and shape, and each has its own personality, from the sparkling bright, to the dark and brooding. The mountains – Skiddaw, Helvellyn, Scafell Pike, Great Gable and many others, not as high or as grand as the Scottish mountains, but perhaps more beautiful in shape and colour – as the peaks form themselves into magnificent groups.

Apart from admiring the beauty of the scenery there is so much to do in the Lake District that the most 'diversified' family will find congenial occupations for every single member.

WALKING

This is probably the finest walking country in England whether for an hour or two, a couple of days, or a fortnight's trek. All are possible and there is freedom of access almost everywhere, though you are asked not to venture into enclosed areas. There are innumerable printed guides to walking tours and short walks, and the Information Centre (address at end of chapter) will supply you with a free list of publications. The National Park organizes guided walks of different lengths from at least nine centres, from about May right through the summer. A free leaflet gives starting times and places (available from Information Centres) and you just join the party.

There are also Nature Trail guide books, available from Information Centres for a small charge, describing trails you can follow all, from different starting places.

FELL WALKING

One of the more exciting adventures for average walkers and families of varying ages over say, ten, is ridge walking in the Lake District. There are many recognized routes, beginning and ending at the same place, which take you along the ridge, giving marvellous views of the peaks and of the well known 'climbing grounds'.

CLIMBING

Rock climbing in the Lake District is for the experienced and not for the casual holidaymaker. But beginners may learn on easy routes with experienced climbers, and some of the climbing clubs give tuition. The best known is the Fell and Rock Climbing Club, who publish comprehensive climbing guides (Cloister Press) to various areas. (Details from the Secretary, F. G. Falkingham, 110 Low Ash Drive, Shipley, West Yorkshire.)

Holiday Courses. Outward Bound Schools run residential holiday courses for boys at Ullswater and Eskdale Green, some for fourteen- to sixteen-year-olds, others for sixteen- to twenty-year-olds. There is also a mixed course for boys and girls in August. All details from Outward Bound Trust, 34 Broadway, London, SW1H 0BQ.

Ramblers' Association Services Ltd have five-day holidays of 'conducted mountain walks' for adults and children over sixteen, at Hasness, Buttermere. Accommodation is in shared rooms, prices from £21 to £26 a week. Bookings with them at Bridge Road East, Welwyn Garden City, Hertfordshire, telephone Welwyn 31133.

The Youth Hostels Association runs 'adventure' holidays for different ages, eleven to fifteen and sixteen plus, consisting of seven and fourteen days' walking, in different areas of the Lake District in July and August. Details from YHA, Trevelyan House, St Albans, Hertfordshire AL1 2DY.

At Storrs Hall Hotel, Windermere, Cumbria, the Sports Council runs weekly courses in fell walking from May to September for those aged seventeen plus to fifty. Accommodation is in a large chalet, in small rooms with double bunks. From £35 per week.

PONY TREKKING AND RIDING

This is excellent country for riding and pony trekking as more than thirty riding centres in and around the Lake District prove. In the National Park, the Lake District Leisure Pursuits Centre, Rayrigg Road, Windermere, Cumbria, approved by 'Ponies of Britain', runs a trekking centre.

Pony trekking residential holidays are organized by at least six different bodies and a booklet, 'Tourist Board Guide to Leisure Pursuits', price 30p, from the Cumbria Tourist Board, Ellerthwaite, Windermere, Cumbria, gives you all relevant information. For a free list of riding centres write to the Information Centre, address at end of chapter.

SAILING

There is good sailing on Windermere and on Ullswater. Two free leaflets from the Information Centre (address at end of chapter) give you important information about moorings, trailers, boat hire and water skiing on Windermere and Ullswater.

Sailing Courses. At Storrs Hall Hotel, Windermere, Cumbria, the Sports Council runs one-week sailing courses mainly for individuals, from the end of May to the end of September for those aged seven to fifty. Price about £37·50 per week (RYA approved).

The Ullswater Sailing School runs weekly and weekend courses from April to September, for individuals and for groups up to ten; the age limit is ten plus for unaccom-

panied children. Price on application from Landends,
Watermillock, near Penrith, Cumbria.

CANOEING

Canoeing is permitted on most of the lakes, except those
that are reservoirs. Windermere, Buttermere, Coniston
Water, Ullswater, Derwentwater, Grasmere and Rydal
Water are open to canoeists. For the others you must
ask permission from the landowner; addresses and free
leaflets from the Information Centre (see end of chapter).
It is *not* possible to hire canoes in the area.

Canoeing Holiday Courses. There are several available.
The Lake District Leisure Pursuits Centre runs group
courses in canoeing as part of their activities programme.
A week's holiday with board and lodging is about £38·03
all equipment provided.

There are also weekly Adventure Sports Holidays for
children, ages nine to thirteen, and thirteen to seventeen,
which give tuition in sailing, canoeing and water skiing.
Details and prices from Lake District Leisure Pursuits
Centre (address p. 82).

The Outward Bound School at Eskdale Green, near
Holmrook, also runs courses in canoeing for boys or men
only and a mixed course for boys and girls in August.
Details from Outward Bound Trust, 34 Broadway,
London SW1H 0BQ.

BOATING

There are facilities for rowing on many of the lakes and
boats are available for hire. Free leaflets are available
from Information Centres, giving details of both rowing
and self-drive motor boating.

WATER SKIING

Water skiing is permitted on some of the lakes though on others the use of speed boats is strictly controlled or forbidden.

BIRDWATCHING

There are said to be 262 species in the area; the wide range of habitat produces a great variety of birds. A leaflet, 'Birds and their Habitats', is available from the Information Centre, address at end of chapter.

ANGLING

Fishing is good and plentiful, but licences and permits are absolutely essential and the authority issuing licences differs with the various areas. The leaflet 'Fishing', available free from Information Centres, gives you all the necessary information including a list of licence distributors. You can find char, eels, perch, pike, brown trout, sea trout and salmon in many of the lakes and rivers.

GLIDING

Good gliding at Walney Airfield, Barrow-in-Furness, Cumbria (outside the National Park). For details of holiday courses contact the Hon. Secretary of the Lakes Gliding Club, Mr R. French, 11a French Street, Barrow-in-Furness, Cumbria.

ARCHAEOLOGY

There is a certain amount of archaeological interest within the National Park, including great stone circles at Castlerigg near Keswick and at Swinside north of Millom. There are two large Iron Age hill forts, and a

considerable number of Roman remains, including a
Roman fort at Hardknott Pass. The relevant chapter in
the *Lake District National Park Guide*, HMSO, price 75p,
makes interesting reading.

ACCOMMODATION

There are many hotels and guest houses throughout the
National Park as well as more specialized accommodation. The National Trust, for example, owns a large part
of the Lake District and rents out accommodation with
self-catering facilities. Their leaflet, 'Self-catering Facilities', is available free from Broadlands, Borrans Road,
Ambleside LA22 0EJ, telephone Ambleside 3003.
Letting is not restricted to National Trust members.

Holiday caravans to house the family are for hire at
Fallbarrow Park. All details from Lake District Leisure
Pursuits Centre (address p. 82).

Camping sites are detailed in a list which is available
from the National Park Information Centre (address at
end of chapter).

There are twenty-nine Youth Hostels in or near the
National Park. Further details from Lakeland Regional
Office, Elleray, Church Street, Windermere LA23 1AW
(telephone Windermere 2301), or from YHA, Trevelyan
House, St Albans, Hertfordshire AL1 2DY (telephone
St Albans 55215).

INFORMATION CENTRES

The National Park Centre at Brockhole, Windermere, has
gardens and picnic grounds as well as an exhibition on
the Lake District together with talks and films. It is open
all year round, admission 11p for adults and 5p for
children up to eighteen. Other Information Centres are
normally open daily from Easter to September. Moot
Hall, Keswick (Keswick 72803). The Barns, Seatoller,

Borrowdale. Old Courthouse, Church Street, Ambleside (Ambleside 3084). Accommodation Bureau (Ambleside 2582). Mobile Units at Glenridding Car Park (mid-summer only) and at Waterhead and Hawkshead Car Parks. Bowness Bay, Bowness-on-Windermere (Windermere 2895) includes an Accommodation Bureau, telephone Windermere 2244.

All written enquiries to Information Officer and Head Warden, District Bank House, High Street, Windermere, Cumbria LA2 3AF.

ACCESS

British Rail takes you to Windermere by branch line from Oxenholme. From Penrith there are good road services to all areas of the Park not served by rail, the main centres being Ambleside, Keswick and Windermere. You can get the following timetables free from the Information Centre (address above): Ravenglass and Eskdale Railway Timetable, and Lakeside Railway Timetable.

6. Northumberland National Park

The Park itself is 398 square miles of wild border country, of moorland, bog and hills, rivers and burns, a landscape of muted colours with hovering kestrels and wheeling curlews high in the sky. It stretches from the Cheviot Hills in the north to the Roman Wall in the south, is bordered by the Forest Park on the west while on the east it takes in the Simonside Hills where rock climbers try their skill on the sandstone crags.

Crawling along for seventy-three miles (fifteen in the Park itself) is the great stone caterpillar of Hadrian's Wall, which dominates the south of the Park.

On the western edge of the Park and partly in Cumbria, the Border Forest Park, run by the Forestry Commission, covers 228 square miles with conifers of different kinds. Many of its broad walks are open to the public and a large area is accessible by car.

Intruding into the centre of the Park is the War Department's All Arms range, between Redesdale and Coquetdale, vast moorland where red 'keep out' flags are flown during firing sessions. It does not affect the landscape, though it does restrict your activities to some extent at certain times.

About thirty or so miles east of the Park, and not to be missed, is the Northumbrian coast, part of which, from Amble to Tweedmouth, has been designated an Area of Outstanding Natural Beauty. Here are wide sandy bays and beaches, good sailing and swimming, a Nature Reserve on the Farne Islands, and at low tide you can drive across the causeway to Lindisfarne, that strange Holy Island where in the seventh century St Cuthbert and St Aidan lived and where you can still see the ruins of the Norman priory.

WALKING

The Pennine Way long-distance footpath runs for the last quarter of its length – about sixty miles – through the Park, coming in at Greenhead in the south-west and going out over the Cheviots, to Scotland. It is tough walking, even for the initiated.

But there are much less strenuous walks for the easygoing, from three miles to ten or twenty, through all kinds of country – green valleys, heathery moorland and along the Roman Wall itself, where you stride along on top of the world viewing the splendid countryside to right and left. Or you can walk along the ridge routes in the Cheviots and across the border, or follow the burns, pool by pool, up the valleys. Or you can follow the Nature Trails which the Park organizes. There are three a year, and each trail runs for six weeks, starting about the middle of May till the end of September.

You can do lovely walks too in the Kielder Forest. There is an Information Centre (and tea room) at Kielder Castle, accessible by car, where you can find out about all the walks you can do in the vast area of the Forest. There is also a camping site and picnic sites in the Forest, and a nature museum.

PONY TREKKING

Pony trekking and riding are at their best in the Park, which has probably the most remote tracts of country in England. You can ride over moor and fell and follow forest trails. Trekking centres are at Hexham, in the Tyne Valley and at Wooler; details from Information Centres (see end of chapter).

ANGLING

Fishing in Northumbria is mostly for salmon, sea trout and brown trout, and is exceptionally good. Most of the fishing in the Park is privately owned, but some hotels have stretches of water for visitors and some clubs accept temporary members on day or weekly tickets. A handbook, produced by the Northumbrian Anglers' Federation, gives you full details of the fishing available. You can get it from the Hon. Secretary, C. Wade, 2 Ridge Villas, Bedlington, Northumberland. The River Tweed is famous for its salmon, and its tributary the Till for its sea trout, which are said to reach the 15–20 lb mark. Salmon fishing on the Coquet (pronounced Coaket) is said to be the cheapest in the country, and the Wear, the largest river in Durham, is good for sea trout. Coarse fishing is to be had on the Tyne and Till, and on the Derwent Reservoir there is 'Fly Only' fishing.

River Board licences are not needed for fishing in the rivers Till, Glen and Bowmont which come under Scottish authority. Rod licences are obtainable from the Northumbrian River Authority, Eldon House, Regent Centre, Gosforth, Newcastle-upon-Tyne NE3 3EX.

ROCK CLIMBING

It is an excellent area for rock climbing with varied terrain of granite, sandstone and basalt. The rocks above Crag Lough on Whin Sill are popular, where the High Shield crag provides about eighty routes of varying difficulty. The sandstone outcrop at Simonside is good for beginners. Good rock climbing, too, in the Cheviots on the Henhole. Further details from Northumbrian Mountaineering Club, H. B. Smith, 27 Bluebell Close, Wylam, Northumberland. The Club also publishes a guide, *Northumberland – a Rock Climbing Guide*, price £1·75.

WILD LIFE

There are badgers, foxes, roe deer, the now rare, red squirrel and the otter, but you have to be sharp-eyed to catch a glimpse of them.

Birds. Bird life is prolific in all areas of the Park, on the moors, in the woods, by the rivers. Some of the more notable are the golden eagle (rare), buzzard, goosander, heron, dipper, green woodpecker, red flycatcher, nightjar and ring ousel. The curlew, whose call can be heard over the moors, has been adopted as the Park's emblem.

ARCHAEOLOGY

Although there are prehistoric burial monuments of the Neolithic era and many relics of the Iron Age, the main interest of the Park lies in the famous Roman remains –

some of which, notably at Vindolanda, are still being excavated – and, of course, the Roman Wall. The Wall, now about seven to eight feet high, is made of huge squares of sandstone quarried locally and filled with rubble in between. It is wide enough to walk along in single file. You can see at intervals the ruins of forts and turrets, and, marking every Roman mile, a mile castle – the remains of one can be seen north of Haltwhistle – while defensive ditches run along either side of its entire length. For a quick, comprehensive look, visit House-steads, where there is a large Roman fort, a mile castle nearby and a fine three-and-a-half-mile sector of the Wall. A useful booklet is 'A Guide to the Roman Wall', by R. G. Collingwood (6th edition) price 15p. A free leaflet, 'The Roman Wall', is available from Information Centres (see end of chapter).

GLIDING

For gliding enthusiasts, the Northumbria Gliding Club, Currock Hill, Chopwell, Newcastle-upon-Tyne NE17 7AV, runs holiday courses from June to September. Temporary membership costs £3.

CAMPING, CARAVANNING AND ACCOMMODATION

There is a fairly good scattering of camping and caravan sites over the Park and the Northumbria Tourist Board, Prudential Building, 140 Pilgrim Street, Newcastle-upon-Tyne, NE1 6TH, gives details of them in a complete 'Register of Accommodation' (free) which also includes hotels and guest houses, furnished accommodation and farmhouses. Youth Hostels are at Wooler, Alnwick, Nine Banks, Otterburn, Bellingham, Hexham, Once Brewed and Byrness. Details from Youth Hostels Association, address on p. 59, or from Information Centres.

INFORMATION CENTRES

Information Centres at Ingram, Once Brewed, Bardon Mill, Byrness, Hexham. Written enquiries to National Park Officer, Bede House, All Saints Centre, Newcastle-upon-Tyne, NE1 2DH.

MOTORING

The 398 square miles of the National Park are laced with narrow roads which are ideal for sightseeing motorists as they are unsuitable for fast driving and are never really crowded. In the off-peak seasons they are positively lonely and remote.

DAY OUTINGS AND WEEKENDS

There are good rail and air services to Newcastle (which is the gateway, as it were, both to the Park and to the coast). Fast rail services from London and Edinburgh and places in between. By air from London to Newcastle takes an hour. A busy diesel service between Newcastle and Carlisle serves the Roman Wall country. (For excursion and weekend fares enquire at any British Rail booking office.) By road, Leeds, York, Carlisle and Berwick are all under 100 miles from Newcastle; Manchester, Glasgow, Edinburgh, Lincoln, Liverpool, Birmingham under 200. There are good coach services from many of these places. Day outings and weekends are therefore feasible from almost the whole of the northern half of England and the southern half of Scotland.

FURTHER REFERENCE

Northumberland National Park Guide, No. 7, price 37½p from the National Park Officer, address as above, or HM Stationery Office, 49 High Holborn, London WC1V 6HB.

7. North York Moors National Park

Walking. Angling. Gliding. Swimming. Pony Trekking and Riding. Archaeology. Geology. Accommodation. Books. Information Centres. Day Outings and Weekends.

This Park is 553 square miles of varied and beautiful landscape set in the north-east corner of Yorkshire. On the coast from Staithes to Scalby, skirting Whitby and Scarborough you get a rugged cliff-line with fishing villages set down in the most unlikely places. Inland in the centre of the Park is a 1200-foot-high plateau of open moorland, remote and solitary, the home of the curlew. red grouse and lapwing. To the north-west are the Cleveland Hills, storehouse of iron, where you can also see spoil heaps of jet workings, the semi-precious stone from which the Romans made ornaments nineteen hundred years ago.

Round the fringes of the moors are the lovely Dales of the south with their woods and ancient villages.

WALKING

Good walking over the moors and along the coast. The Cleveland Way (see page 60) runs mostly within the Park. A number of free leaflets describing short walks are available from the Park Department (see address at end of chapter). Long-distance walkers should be prepared for sudden mists and changes in weather.

ANGLING

Fishing for trout and grayling in the Rye and Derwent and for salmon and trout in the Esk. Most of the water is private and details of permits, licences and addresses are given in the *Northern Anglers' Handbook*, the Dalesman Publishing Co. Ltd, Clapham via Lancaster, North Yorkshire, price 49p including postage.

GLIDING

Visitors are accepted on courses at Sutton Bank. Contact Yorkshire Gliding Club, Sutton Bank, Thirsk, for further details. There is also weekends-only gliding at Carlton Moor, Carlton in Cleveland, Middlesbrough, Cleveland, where the Newcastle and Teesside Gliding Club operates.

SWIMMING

Most of the coast is cliff and fairly rugged, but there are

good safe beaches at Whitby and Scarborough, both
just outside the Park area.

PONY TREKKING AND RIDING

The Park is good riding country and there are stables all
over the area. Five-day and eight-day holidays are run
by Ryedale Travel Agency, 8 Bondgate, Helmsley,
York YO6 5BT, based on two hotels in Helmsley and a
Youth Hostel. There are also many riding centres and
you can get a list of names and addresses of stables
around Scarborough from the Information Centre, St
Nicholas Cliff, Scarborough.

ARCHAEOLOGY

There are many groups of small cairns and burial mounds
in the area and large barrows known as 'howes'. Not many
Roman remains but a well-preserved stretch of Roman
road called 'Wade's Causeway' on Wheeldale Moor runs
from near Goathland towards Snape.

GEOLOGY

Those interested in geology will want to read the chapter
by Professor Hemingway in the *North York Moors
National Park Guide*, price 45p, in which he traces the
Park's exceptional geological history, starting with
Jurassic times, about 180 million years ago.

ACCOMMODATION

The Park Information Service does not publish a register
of accommodation but you can get from them (address
at end of chapter) a free leaflet entitled 'Accommodation
in the Moors' which gives a list of addresses to write to.
This leaflet also lists Caravan and Camp Sites with names
and addresses; and the Yorkshire Tourist Board publish

a booklet which gives full details of most of the sites open to touring campers and caravanners, available from the Board at 312 Tadcaster Road, York, telephone York 67961. There are also Youth Hostels at Wheeldale, Westerdale, Helmsley, Scalby Mills, Whitby, Boggle Hole (near Robin Hood's Bay) and Saltburn.

BOOKS

North York Moors National Park (HMSO, 45p) gives information on the background of the Park. *North York Moors Tourist Map* (HMSO, price 55p). A free leaflet available from the National Park Department (address below) gives a book list of guides to forest trails, historical monuments, museums, walks, motor drives etc.

INFORMATION CENTRES

North York Moors National Park Department, The Old Vicarage, Bondgate, Helmsley, North Yorkshire. This is the only centre, but the Forestry Commission have a Trailside Museum Information Centre at Low Dalby north of Thornton Dale.

DAY OUTINGS AND WEEKENDS

The Park is easily accessible by road for day outings from some of the big northern cities; Manchester is 91 miles from Helmsley, Newcastle, 64, York 24, and Liverpool 120. For weekends, Helmsley and the surrounding country is 175 miles from Edinburgh, 181 from Cambridge, and 220 miles from London.

8. Peak District

Walking, Riding and Pony Trekking.   Rock Climbing.
Caving and Potholing.   Archaeology.   Geology.   Angling.
Birdwatching.   Canoeing.   Holiday Centre.   Camping
and Caravanning.   Information Centre.   Day Outings
and Weekends.

The Peak District is made up of 524 square miles of
wooded dales with clear running rivers, bleak moorland
and high green plateaux, of which more than half are in
Derbyshire extending into Cheshire, Staffordshire, Greater Manchester and South and West Yorkshire. This
wonderful stretch of romantic landscape, with its under-
tones of melancholy, is set in the very heart of industrial
England and is within about a fifty-mile reach of seventeen million people. Even so, it does not appear to
become overcrowded.

The main charm of the Park lies in its infinite variety. This is because of its geological structure which produces distinct and quite individual types of landscape within the area and at the same time makes the Park ideal for a family holiday since there are so many different activities available: rock climbing and hill walking in the northern area around the massive Kinder Scout and Bleaklow (2000 feet up) and on the initial stages of the Pennine Way; potholing and caving in the limestone country round Castleton; fishing and sometimes canoeing in the valleys of the Derwent, Wye and Dove; walking and riding over almost all the Park, but especially in the green dales of Dovedale and the Manifold valley.

WALKING, RIDING AND PONY TREKKING

There is excellent walking everywhere, although walkers are required to keep to the footpaths since most of the Park is privately owned. For the single-minded enthusiast of the 'rambler' class, the High Peak in the North is exciting in all weathers.

The plateaux of Kinder Scout – Bleaklow, Black Hill – at 2000 feet are wild and peat-covered with deep cloughs and sudden cliffs or 'edges', tors and waterfalls. The going is tough, and compass and maps are essential, as there are not many tracks. For the less ambitious there is lovely easy walking further south in the White Peak limestone uplands, with excellent paths and bridleways, some of them dating back to pre-Roman times. The Tissington Trail, thirteen miles of greenway, opened in 1972, follows the old railway line between Ashbourne and Parsley Hay. Linking up with it at Parsley Hay is the High Peak trail, running for seventeen miles through the gentle woods of the Derwent valley to the windy uplands of the High Peak. Both trails are open to walkers, cyclists and horse-riders. A leaflet, 'Riding in the Peak National Park', is available, price 3p plus 5½p postage, from the Information Centre (see end of chapter).

ROCK CLIMBING

Gritstone edges and limestone cliffs are the Peak's special features and are particularly good for beginners as they are only moderately high – up to 100 feet. For experienced climbers there are also the vertical faces which test varying degrees of skill. Climbs on the limestone cliffs are longer and harder.

CAVING AND POTHOLING

For the adventurous there are great opportunities for exploring caves and underground passages in the limestone area of the Peak, and this goes on all the year round. Some caverns are equipped with boats etc. for the tourist and are worth a visit for the very weirdness of their beauty. But the serious potholer puts on his tin hat with its light on top and explores the lesser known caves along with his friends, never alone, a difficult and sometimes dangerous sport, demanding skill and teamwork.

ARCHAEOLOGY

There are Megalithic monuments, Iron Age hillforts and burial mounds in the area, as well as prehistoric implements, Roman roads and forts and Saxon crosses – in fact much to interest the archaeologist.

GEOLOGY

The Peak is rich in minerals and a good area for the holidaying geologist. There are some remarkable rocks to be seen in the limestone area, Ilam Rock in Dovedale, Lion Rock, the Dove Holes and others. Lead was worked in Derbyshire in Roman times, and the famous Blue John used for making ornaments is still mined near Castleton.

ANGLING

The clear waters of the Dove, where Izaak Walton used to fish, are renowned for trout and grayling as are the Derwent and the Wye and their tributaries. Much of the water is privately owned by clubs but some stretches of river belong to hotels for the use of visitors. (You can get details from the Peak National Park Office, address at end of chapter.) There is also some coarse fishing on the Derwent.

BIRDWATCHING

This is a fine area for birdwatchers. Birds to look out for on the high moors, are the red grouse, merlin, golden plover, curlew, dunlin, common sandpiper, twite, dipper, and ring ousel. In the dales, redstart, tree pipit, wood warbler; and in the valleys, marsh tit, long-tailed tit, tree creeper and wheatear. Also snipe, skylark, yellow hammer, nightjar and kingfisher.

CANOEING

Canoeing throughout England and Wales is deeply involved with fishing rights and since river waters are mostly privately owned canoeing is not likely to be permitted where there is fishing. There are several rivers in the Peak District suitable for canoeing and to find out where it is allowed, contact the British Canoe Union, 70 Brompton Road, London SW3 1DT, referring them to the area you are interested in. Or write to Derbyshire Canoe Association, Mr F. Booth, Kyloe Cottage, Sutton Scarsdale, near Chesterfield.

HOLIDAY CENTRE

The Peak District National Park has a Residential Centre at Losehill Hall, Castleton, with accommodation for sixty people in single and double rooms and family suites. Courses are open to all, with much outdoor activity on such subjects as birdwatching, rambles in the Peak, landscape painting and photography, geology, architecture and prehistory of the Peak. Charges are reasonable. Enquiries to the Principal, Losehill Hall, Castleton, Sheffield S30 2WB.

CAMPING AND CARAVANNING

There are many camping and caravan sites round and about the National Park. For details of approved sites write to Peak National Park Office (see end of chapter) or the recognized camping and caravanning clubs. There are fifteeen Youth Hostels (addresses from Peak National Park Office or Youth Hostels Association (address p. 59). Accommodation in hotels and guest houses is of a good standard, but booking in advance is essential in the high season.

INFORMATION CENTRE

For personal callers, The Market Hall, Bridge Street, Bakewell. Written enquiries to Peak National Park Office, Baslow Road, Bakewell, Derbyshire DE4 1AE.

DAY OUTINGS AND WEEKENDS

Since the Peak is surrounded by industrial cities, Manchester, Sheffield, Liverpool, Birmingham etc., all within about eighty or so miles of the Park's beautiful countryside, day outings are practicable for all of the activities already mentioned. From London to Bakewell is a car trip of only 150 miles, which leaves ample time for a weekend of outdoor enjoyment.

9. Pembrokeshire Coast

*Walking. Pony Trekking. Angling. Sailing.
Swimming. Sub-Aqua Swimming. Gliding. Birdwatching. Sea Life. Archaeology. Geology. Countryside Unit. Accommodation. Information Centres.
Day Outings and Weekends.*

This smallest of the National Parks packs into its 225
square miles unbelievable riches for those who spend
their time off there. There are secluded bays and sandy
beaches where you can spend days bathing and picnick-
ing and with luck, see grey seals; there are safe anchor-
ages for small boat sailors and good sea fishing.

The Park has five nature reserves: a Bird Observatory
(residential only) on Skokholm (pronounced Skoakum)
and a nature reserve on Ramsey Island, both run by the
Royal Society for the Protection of Birds; a national
nature reserve on Skomer; the biggest gannet colony in
the world on Grassholm; and a nature reserve on St
Margaret's island belonging to the West Wales Natural-
ists' Trust (permits only).

Within the Park live two distinct communities, the
'Welshery' and the 'Englishery'. In the North the people
are Welsh speaking, occupied mainly with sheep farming
in the hills, and in the other half of the county is 'Little
England beyond Wales', predominantly English speaking, mainly farming the well-cultivated lands of the
south.

The climate is mild. The gulf-stream, or North
Atlantic Drift, sweeping round the coast gives virtually
frost-free winters. The coast area is reasonably dry with
a rainfall of thirty-two inches, compared with eighty

inches in the Presely Hills. But it is also very windy, with thirty-two gales expected a year and fierce winds a normal feature. On the other hand it is sunny on the coast and Dale, near Milford Haven, is said to be the sunniest place in all Wales.

WALKING

The Park's 170 miles of magnificent rocky coast has an 'approved' (i.e. more or less well-kept) long-distance footpath running for its entire length from St Dogmaels in the north to Amroth in the south. The walking is testing but never really difficult; in some places the path gets overgrown but you will have no real problems if you are properly equipped with stout shoes and thornproof trousers – shorts and beach shoes are not adequate. You won't need a compass, but you will certainly need a map. One of the most beautiful stretches of the path is from St David's Peninsula to Neyland near Milford Haven, with seabirds, seals and several islands to contemplate en route. You can get a free leaflet 'Pembrokeshire Coast Path', and a set of five, 3p leaflets covering sections of the path, from the National Park Information Centres (see end of chapter) and from the Countryside Commission, address p. 60. Public transport is not good, so if you don't want to walk back the way you came, get someone to meet you at your destination. It is hoped soon to have access lanes to the Path, making circular walks possible. There are also lovely walks in the nature reserves and summaries of guided walks and lectures are available free. There is also a 'Programme of Guided Walks and Lectures', which give details and dates, price 5p. Both from Information Centres (see end of chapter).

PONY TREKKING

There is good hill walking on the wild and solitary moors of the Presely Hills, which are also specially fitted for

pony trekking since there are practically no roads.
You can often start straight off on the heathery moorland for a day or a half-day's riding. A leaflet, 'Riding
and Pony Trekking', with details of stables and prices is
available from Information Centres.

ANGLING

Good and varied sea fishing; sporting fishing for salmon
and trout; limited coarse fishing. You can get 'Fishing
in Pembrokeshire', a leaflet with addresses for licences,
permits, clubs etc., free from the National Park Information Centres.

SAILING

The Park has some of the most beautiful and safe small
boat sailing in the country and some of the most dangerous. It is perfectly easy, and indeed essential, to find out
which are the dangerous areas and to avoid them.
'Dinghy Sailing in Pembrokeshire', a leaflet, price 3p
from Information Centres, is extremely helpful as it
includes a loose-leaf map marking in red the unsafe
areas and in blue the safe areas, as well as sailing clubs,
dinghy parks etc.

SWIMMING

There are many sheltered sandy beaches, some easier to
get at than others. *Pembrokeshire Coast National Park
Guide*, price 40p, available from Information Centres,
gives a detailed description of almost all the bathing
beaches so that you know whether to expect them to be
crowded or not.

SUB-AQUA SWIMMING

Diving in these waters is superb, according to those

who have done it, especially from Dale Fort, where the Field Centre runs courses in marine biology and underwater photography for trained divers. Enquiries to the Welsh Association of Sub-Aqua Clubs, c/o Dale Fort Field Centre, Dale, Haverfordwest, Dyfed.

GLIDING

The West Wales Gliding Association, Haverfordwest Airport, is open for gliding every weekend and runs weeklong courses at times during the summer months. They accept visitors as temporary members.

BIRDWATCHING

The Park has probably one of the finest concentrations of sea birds anywhere in the country and these are mostly on the off-shore islands of Ramsey, Skomer, Skokholm and Grassholm, all of which are nature reserves. Most of them can be visited by the public, though permits are sometimes required – enquire at Information Centres. Skomer Island, which is fairly large (722 acres), can be reached easily by boat from St Martin's Haven and is well worth a whole day's visit.

SEA LIFE

One of the exceptional sights of this coast is the Atlantic grey seals, which breed on Skomer and on Ramsey Island. They swim close inshore, fish at high tide and bask on the rocks at low tide and it is usually possible to see them from almost any point along the coastline. If you are lucky you may also see dolphins, porpoises and even whales.

ARCHAEOLOGY

Relics of prehistoric man abound in the Park particularly in the Presely Hills from where, it is now accepted, the blue or 'foreign' stones came which are incorporated in the inner circle at Stonehenge. Cromlechau or chambered stone tombs of various kinds are to be found in the north, most famous of which is the Pentre Ifan. There is also GorsFawr, a stone circle near Mynachlog-ddu, many standing stones, Bronze Age barrows, Iron Age earthworks but few, if any, Roman remains. For technical details and history see the *Pembrokeshire Coast National Park Guide*, which has three interesting chapters on the subject. Available from HM Stationery Office, price 75p, or from Information Centres.

GEOLOGY

Geologists find much of interest here, where according to the National Park Guide, 'the rocks reveal a complex history spanning several thousand million years that included ... the repeated folding of the rocks by powerful earth movements and the moulding of a variety of landscapes by erosion.'

COUNTRYSIDE UNIT

At Broadhaven the Countryside Unit is also the principal Information Centre. Lectures and seminars are held there on wild life and there is usually an officer present to answer individual questions.

ACCOMMODATION

The names, addresses and telephone numbers of hotels, guest houses, farm houses and private houses are available from the Information Centres in a free leaflet,

'Accommodation List', which also covers camping and caravan sites. There are also six Youth Hostels, mostly in the north-west, between St Dogmaels and St Davids, with one in the south at Saundersfoot. Additional information from the Youth Hostels Association (for address see p. 59).

INFORMATION CENTRES

The Norton, Tenby; Drill Hall, Main Street, Pembroke; City Hall, St Davids; Town Hall, Fishguard; Countryside Unit, Broad Haven; Kilgetty, Kingsmoor Common; Town Hall, Milford Haven; Castle Museum, Haverfordwest. Written enquiries to County Offices, Haverfordwest, Dyfed.

DAY OUTINGS AND WEEKENDS

The Pembrokeshire Coast National Park has fairly good road and rail links with industrial South Wales while the Midlands and London are a six-hour journey away. From Tenby by road Cardiff is 93 miles, Bristol 125 miles, Birmingham 140, and London 239 miles. So day outings are possible from many industrial areas, and long weekends, if you are keen, from as far away as London.

10. Snowdonia National Park

Walking. Hill Walking. Pony Trekking. Rock Climbing. Angling. Archaeology. Geology. Swimming and Water Skiing. Sailing. Training Centre. Accommodation. Camping and Caravanning. Information Centres. Day Outings and Weekends.

The Park is about 850 square miles of mountains, lakes, rivers, rugged passes, precipices, and green valleys with a stretch of coast in the west from Harlech to Aberdovey. It has been designated an Area of Outstanding Natural Beauty so you can be sure that, wherever you go, the countryside will be surpassingly lovely with a wild and rugged grandeur peculiarly its own.

The Park reaches from near Conwy (Conway) in the north, to the seaport of Aberdovey in the south, bounded on the west by Llanberis, Harlech and Barmouth, and on the east by Llanrwst and Bala; basically country for open-air, active holidays of the walking/climbing/fishing variety with good facilities for camping and caravanning. The two great mountain ranges are centred round Snowdon in the north-west of the area and Cader Idris in the southern half.

For the less energetic members of the family there is no lack of things to do and see: medieval castles to be visited; scores, literally, of ancient monuments – from prehistoric hut circles to Roman remains; many nature reserves as well as forest, farm and nature trails to follow; on Bala's lake there is sailing tuition in dinghies.

With all these attractions Snowdonia National Park tends to be alive with people in the summer except on the dizzy rock faces and in the remote highland passes. And a note about the weather: being a mountainous area, Snowdonia gets more than its fair share of rain – in fact, it can be very wet, so go prepared.

WALKING

Good walking in all areas of the Park on tracks, lanes, old pony routes and footpaths. You can choose between the long, rough, adventurous hill walk (see below) which takes most of the day, and the short two- to three-mile 'landscape trail'. Leaflets of all landscape trails can be had from the Information Centre (address at end of chapter).

HILL WALKING

Snowdonia, with its five northern and three southern ranges of mountains and fourteen peaks over 3000 feet,

is ideal country for the enthusiast who wants something
less arduous than a real climb but more challenging than
a mere walk. The National Park has innumerable walks
of this kind, starting with the traverses of the main sum-
mits and the ridges in each district, walks enough to
keep most people fully exercised. Details of routes from
guide books, and in particular the official National Park
Guide, *Snowdonia*, published by HM Stationery Office,
price 75p.

PONY TREKKING

There is not much pony trekking within the Park compared with the rest of Wales, but there are stables at,
among other places, Llanbedr, Dolgellau, Bala, Beth-
esda and Conwy. Leaflet on pony trekking in Wales
from the Wales Tourist Board, Welcome House, High
Street, Llandaff, Cardiff, CF5 2YZ.

ROCK CLIMBING

All kinds of rock climbing for all grades of climbers with
areas suitable for the beginner, and the hardest and
steepest climbs in the country for the expert. For those
in between there are many long routes which, though
not over-difficult, call for climbing knowledge and
ability to spot bad rock, and they do eventually take you
to a mountain top. Climbing is centred on the Nant
Ffrancon Pass in the Glyder range and Llanberis Pass,
both to the north of Snowdon. Most climbers stay at one
or other place; there is a newish Youth Hostel at Pen-y-
Pass at the head of Llanberis Pass.

ANGLING

In a countryside laced with rivers there is plenty of good
fishing but first you must get a permit from the angling
club, association, or syndicate in whose waters you

intend to fish, or the permission of the river owner or occupier, as well as a licence issued by the Wales Water Resources Board. Club permits and Board licences can be had from some sub post offices, fishing tackle dealers and sports shops.

There is salmon, sea trout and brown trout fishing in many rivers; and brown trout and char are to be had in a large number of lakes.

Full details of fishing available to visitors can be had from the Gwynedd River Division, Highfield, St David's Road, Caernarvon, or the Dee & Clwyd River Division, 2 Vicar's Lane, Chester. Details of fishing and boating on Llyn Tegid are available from the Lake Warden, 24 Ffordd Pensarn, Bala.

ARCHAEOLOGY

There are many ancient monuments from round barrows of the Bronze Age to hut circles of the Iron Age, Roman forts, camps and settlements.

GEOLOGY

The complex geological structure of North Wales has interested geologists, including Darwin, over the ages, and research has produced considerable detailed information. Much of the rock fabric is clearly exposed to view. See *National Park Guide, Snowdonia.*

SWIMMING AND WATER SKIING

Long, safe beaches from Harlech Point along the coast to Aberdovey. Water skiing also at Aberdovey.

SAILING

Good sailing in the estuaries of the Dovey at Aberdovey, the Mawddach at Barmouth, the Artro at Llanbedr and Pensarn and the Conwy at Conwy. Most sailing clubs

accept temporary members. At Bala the Youth Hostels
Association runs a sailing tuition centre on the four-mile
lake. Age limit is sixteen, with a special course for children from eleven to fifteen. Details from Youth Hostels
Association (address p. 59). For names and addresses of
sailing clubs see leaflet, 'Sailing and Water Sports',
available free, from Wales Tourist Board, address below.

TRAINING CENTRE

Plas y Brenin National Mountaineering Centre is run by
the Sports Council at Capel Curig and offers a wide choice
of one-week courses for people over seventeen. These
cover most aspects of mountaineering from mountain
navigation, walking, camping, to snow and ice climbing.
Courses too in skiing (artificial ski slope), orienteering,
canoeing and expedition photography. Prices vary
according to the subject but £25 to £30 a week is about
normal. For booking write to Sports Council (Dept. B),
70 Brompton Road, London SW3 1EX.

ACCOMMODATION

Guest houses and hotels in and round the Park and
seventeen Youth Hostels. The Snowdonia National Park
Committee run 'look after yourself' chalets to sleep four
at Llanrwst. Details from Snowdonia National Park
Countryside Centre, Glan-y-Borth, Llanrwst.

CAMPING AND CARAVANNING

There are sites in and around centres like Harlech,
Dolgellau, Llanrwst, Bangor and Caernarvon. Bookings
should be arranged beforehand direct with the private
owners. Details from the Wales Tourist Board, Welcome
House, High Street, Llandaff, Cardiff CF5 2YZ.

These centres are open continuously from **Easter to the end of September** at Llanrwst, Glan-y-Borth; Llanberis, Craig Afon, Snowdon Road; Blaenau Ffestiniog, Queen's Bridge; Bala, Old British School; Dolgellau, Bridge End; Harlech; Aberdovey. Written enquiries to Information Centre, Yr Hen Usgol, Maentwrog, Blaenau Ffestiniog, Gwynedd LL41 4HW.

DAY OUTINGS AND WEEKENDS

For day outings by car, Bala and Betws-y-Coed are both within easy reach of Liverpool, Chester, Shrewsbury and Stoke-on-Trent, all of which are under seventy miles from one or other centre. And for a weekend, if you don't mind a longish drive, London (211 miles), Cardiff (171 miles) and Bristol (164 miles), are perfectly feasible, too.

11. Yorkshire Dales

Walking. Angling. Birdwatching. Archaeology.
Caving and Potholing. Accommodation. Camping.
Caravanning. Information Centres. Day Outings and
Weekends.

The Park is 680 square miles of hill and dale, mountain
and river in the north-west of Yorkshire. It straddles
the Pennines – the watershed of the North – and five
rivers; four of them, the Swale, Ure, Aire and Wharfe
flow into the North Sea, while the Ribble flows west to
the Irish Sea. And it is the valleys of these rivers that
form the Dales.

The charm of the Dales is the variety of their landscape, from narrow, craggy ravines to spacious green
valleys. A feature of the landscape is the waterfalls,
locally known as 'forces' and well worth a visit: Hardraw
near Hawes, Aysgarth Falls, Waterfalls Walk at Ingleton
– three miles of grandeur – to mention just a few.

There are seven main Dales in the Park and several
other smaller ones. *Garsdale* and *Dentdale* in the remote
north-west of the Park are more intimate valleys less
visited by tourists than, say, *Ribblesdale*, which includes
the Three Peaks of Ingleborough, Whernside and Pen y
Ghent – Great Scar Limestone country. *Wharfedale* is
thought by some to be the loveliest. *Swaledale* in the
north-east of the Park has steep fells and rugged gorges.
Wensleydale is broad and spacious, rich in dairy farm
land, whence comes the cheese. In *Malhamdale* at the
head of the river Aire, is Malham Cove, a massive vertical
exposure of the Great Scar Limestone, and Gordale Scar,
a sinister and rugged gorge of great interest to geologists.

WALKING

The Pennine Way (see Part 2, Chapter 1) runs through
the Park, but that is really tough going even for people
in the 'rambler' class. For the less hardy there are miles
and miles of footpaths and in many of the villages maps
show the rights of way. Leaflets are available free from
Information Centres (see end of chapter), also a very useful book list (Broadsheet No. 8) covering all aspects of the
Park. There is very little, if any, pony trekking.

ANGLING

There is good fishing everywhere, for trout and for coarse
fish. Most of the best water is private but certain stretches
belong to angling clubs, a few of which issue day tickets.
It is essential to have a rod licence from the River
Board and the permission of the owner of the fishing

rights before you start. You can find all details of where to fish, in the *Northern Anglers' Handbook*, published by Dalesman Publishing Co. Ltd, Clapham, via Lancaster, price 49p including postage.

BIRDWATCHING

The Dales are particularly rich in bird life and you can get a check list from the Information Centres which names more than 140 different kinds of birds from the bullfinch to the black-necked grebe and the waxwing.

ARCHAEOLOGY

There is much to interest the archaeologist: burial mounds and Megalithic monuments, early Bronze Age earthworks known as 'henges' and Roman remains.

CAVING AND POTHOLING

Yorkshire is the great caving area of England and cave systems are continually being extended by exploration. In the National Park, most potholing and caving is centred round the Three Peaks (Ingleborough, Whernside and Pen y Ghent). At Whernside Manor, Dent, the National Scout Caving Centre runs caving courses for boys, see p. 31. You do not have to be a member of the Scouts, though preference is given to them (see p. 123). Another caving centre is Upper Wharfedale. For information write to the Hon. Secretary, Council of Northern Caving Clubs, 6 Monkroyd Avenue, Barnoldswick, via Colne, Lancashire.

Non-cavers can visit the show caves, which are lighted, at Ingleborough Cave, Clapham, White Scar Cave and Stump Cross. At Selside you can visit the spectacular entrance to Alum Pot, one of the great potholes of the Dales.

ACCOMMODATION

For hotels, guest houses and furnished accommodation –
houses, cottages, etc. – contact Yorkshire Dales Tourist
Association, Burnsall, via Skipton, North Yorkshire, for
an accommodation list. There are ten Youth Hostels in
the area and others which serve the Park. Enquiries to
Youth Hostels Association Headquarters for the area at
96 Main Street, Bingley, West Yorkshire.

CAMPING

There are a few sites in the Park which are listed in the
Yorkshire Dales Official Guide and Handbook, published
by the Yorkshire Dales Tourist Association (address
above). Many farmers not listed will welcome those visitors who ask for permission to camp. No services are
provided and you have to cope with water and sanitary
arrangements yourself.

CARAVANNING

There are some sites for touring caravans within the Park
and others within easy motoring distance. These, too,
are listed in the *Yorkshire Dales Official Guide and Handbook* (see above). Advance booking is advisable.

INFORMATION CENTRES

Aysgarth Falls in Wensleydale; Clapham between Settle
and Ingleton; Malham at the head of the river Aire.
For written enquiries apply to Information Service,
Colvend House, Hebden Road, Grassington, Skipton,
North Yorkshire.

DAY OUTINGS AND WEEKENDS

The Yorkshire Dales National Park is ideally situated for

day outings from the surrounding industrial country, for example, Blackburn, Bradford, Burnley, Halifax, Harrogate, Lancaster, Leeds, Preston, York, Manchester and Sheffield are all under sixty miles from Skipton by road.

For weekends in the Park, Birmingham is 142 miles from Skipton while London is 214 miles.

12. Children on Their Own

Youth Hostels Association.   Scouts.   Girl Guides.
Outward Bound.   Other Holidays.

Every year sees a greater variety of organized holidays
available for children without their parents, which is
probably a good thing from everyone's point of view.
All sorts of organizations, commercial and otherwise, run
all kinds of courses in all kinds of places – pony trekking,
canoeing, climbing, photography, underwater swimming,
caving, cycling and so on.

YOUTH HOSTELS ASSOCIATION

The biggest choice probably comes from the Youth
Hostels Association, which is a non-profit-making organ-
ization and which the children must join if they want to
take advantage of YHA holidays. For details of membership fees see p. 59.

For eleven- to fifteen-year-olds the YHA run Eagle
Adventure Holidays, some for boys and girls separately
and some mixed.

Walking Holidays.   The most popular are usually for
seven days and mostly for girls only or boys only, in
charge of an experienced leader. Walks cover moderate
distances which any reasonably fit child can manage.
Costs for a seven-day walking holiday are about £22.
Parents must get children to the assembly point and
pick them up, or make arrangements for them, at the end

of the trip. Walking holidays cover beautiful country including Snowdonia, the Yorkshire Dales, Mendips, Isle of Man, Dorset, South Devon Coast and so on.

Cycling. Holidays arranged by the YHA in collaboration with the Cyclists' Touring Club cover moderate distances leaving time to stop off and explore interesting places. Any bicycle is acceptable but it must be in good condition. There are about ten different tours to choose from.

Canoe Training. Canoe training down the Wye from Staunton to Chepstow, ages twelve to fifteen only.

Sailing. A week's sailing on Lake Bala, North Wales.

Riding. At various places, including the Cotswolds.

Birdwatching. Birdwatching in charge of an ornithologist and a YHA leader.

Combined Activity Courses. There are 'Combined Activity' Courses where members of the Young Ornithologists Club combine birdwatching with, say, canoeing, sailing and rock climbing.

For boys and girls aged sixteen and over there is an even wider range of holidays, and groups are of both sexes. Their holidays have a more adult slant. Costs for a week vary with the kind of holiday and the facilities involved, from about £22 to about £48. But for each holiday the price covers accommodation and all food, plus fares for excursions and bus travel included in the programme and a small charge for insurance. Full details from YHA Adventure Holidays, Trevelyan House, St Albans, Hertfordshire AL1 2DY.

SCOUTS

Scouts run all kinds of holidays for their members all the

year round. There are national camp sites in Kent,
Sussex, Surrey, Hertfordshire, Oxford and one in the
Lake District at Windermere. Camps are open all the
year and each has its individual attraction, whether it is
a swimming pool, sports field, winter cabin or other
amenity. There are also three National Activity Centres –
one for *Boating* at Marlow, Buckinghamshire, an *Air*
centre at Lasham Airfield, near Alton, Hampshire, and
a *Caving* centre at Whernside Manor, Dent, via Sedbergh,
Cumbria. The caving centre is also open to anyone interested in caving; age is usually restricted to over sixteen,
though special arrangements can be made for younger
children. Week-end caving courses for beginners are also
arranged at the centre.

Air Activity Centre. At the Air Activity Centre there
are many courses to choose from, including Air Adventure
Weekends for boys of twelve to sixteen. This course introduces the Scout to ballooning, parascending, etc. There
are also week-long Air Adventure Camps, which continue
the instruction given on the weekend courses.

Rowing, canoeing and sailing. For this Scouts go to the
Longridge Activity Centre near Marlow, Buckinghamshire, where there are eight acres of open ground along
the Thames. All sorts of craft are available and there is a
staff to assist in training. Scouts have to be able to swim
at least fifty yards, clothed, before they can join a course.
This Centre is also open to non-Scouts.

Costs of courses are moderate, though they vary
according to the equipment involved. Most weekend
courses cost £8, at least, per person depending on the
activity involved. Local Education Authorities are often
prepared to consider applications for grant aid for boys
of fourteen and over to take part in courses at training
centres.

For full details of the Scout Movement and holiday courses write to the Scout Association, Baden-Powell House, Queensgate, London SW7 5JS.

GIRL GUIDES

Girl Guides are more decentralized than the Scouts and their plans for Guider and Ranger camps, Brownie Pack holidays and other holidays are usually made at local level. But there are outdoor Activity Centres in all the six regions of England, and also in Scotland, Wales and Northern Ireland, where members can enjoy all kinds of outdoor pursuits geared to the countryside surrounding the centre. For example, 'Adventure' courses for thirteen- to fifteen-year-olds include pony trekking, canoeing, hill walking, swimming and orienteering or a selection of these, while some of the winter courses for Rangers and Guides may offer folk lore, folk crafts and learning the guitar.

For further details write to the Girl Guides Association, 17–19 Buckingham Palace Road, London SW1W 0PT.

OUTWARD BOUND

In spite of the deeper issues underlying the Outward Bound Trust – their motto is 'To serve, to strive and not to yield' – the courses themselves are good fun and much enjoyed by the participants. They are not 'holiday' courses as such but are designed to stimulate, mentally and physically.

Every boy and girl has to have a sponsor, i.e. someone to pay for him/her. This can be a parent, or a child may pay for himself, but most boys and girls are sponsored by industrial and commercial firms or organizations. The person to contact in this respect is the firm's Personnel Manager. Some Local Education Authorities also support the Junior Courses and applications for financial assistance should be made to the child's Headmaster.

Courses are organized for four main groups: Junior, for boys from fourteen to sixteen and girls from fourteen-and-a-half to sixteen; Standard, for boys sixteen to twenty, and a Mixed course for boys and girls from sixteen to twenty; Senior, for boys from twenty upwards. The fee for each course of twenty-six days is £160 (£155 for Girls' Junior Course).

The courses consist of all kinds of different activities of the sailing, mountaineering, swimming, canoeing variety, but also include such subjects as public speaking and discussion groups. There are five schools: two in Wales, two in Cumbria (Cumberland) and one in Morayshire. The girls' school at Tywyn, Gwynedd, includes courses in camping, rock climbing, movement to music, drama and first aid. Full details from Outward Bound Trust, 34 Broadway, London SW1H 0BQ.

OTHER HOLIDAYS

Apart from the holidays provided by these three big organizations, there are literally hundreds of different holidays for children of all ages run by commercial firms, Education Authorities, and children's holiday centres, all over Britain. There are even privately-run seaside holidays for three- to seven-year-olds on their own. It is as well to try to get a personal recommendation for holidays run by firms that you know nothing about.

It is obviously not within the scope of this book to give details of all of them but you may find useful the book *Activity Holidays in England* published by the English Tourist Board, 4 Grosvenor Gardens, London SW1W 0DU, price 60p plus 10p postage. It gives details of holiday courses in different outdoor pursuits for people of all ages, including children, whose holidays are described with age-groups and prices specified. It also covers cultural pursuits – arts festivals, drama summer schools, painting etc.

Holiday Fellowship Ltd., 142 Great North Way, Hendon, London NW4 1EG, runs holidays for unaccompanied children in three age groups – eight to tens, eleven to thirteens, and fourteen to fifteens – at Malhamdale, North Yorkshire, where they enjoy a general outdoor active holiday with games and excursions but no special courses. Cost, £15 per child, per week, inclusive of everything except travel. The older group of fourteen- to seventeen-year-olds can also have an active outdoor holiday at Wye Valley, Monmouthshire or at Newlands, Cumbria, price £15 to £15·50 per week. Specialized activity holidays where you can go pony trekking, birdwatching or on archaeology expeditions, under the guidance of a leader, are also available to fourteen-year-olds and upwards, who may go alone or with older friends or parents. Cost from £20 per week.

Specialized one-week holiday courses with an educational slant are run in the North Yorkshire Moors National Park for children of different age groups from eight years to fourteen. They stay at the Field Centres at Whitby or Scarborough where courses include such subjects as 'Life on the Seashore', ages ten to twelve, or Outdoor Pursuits, for the eight-to-tens. There are many other subjects from 'Riding for Beginners' to the 'Young Angler' and the 'Forest Naturalist'. Holiday courses take place at Easter and in the summer holidays from the middle of July to the end of August. Courses cost from £15 per week including board and lodging but not travel, to about £32, plus VAT, depending on the type of course. All details from the Director, Larpool Hall, Larpool Drive, Whitby, North Yorkshire.

The Council for Colony Holidays for Schoolchildren, Linden Manor, Upper Colwall, Malvern, Worcestershire, runs communal holidays on the lines of the French colonies de vacances at many centres throughout Britain for children aged nine to thirteen. These are for periods of nine, twelve and twenty-five days between mid-July and September. Cost is about £18 for nine days or £59 for twenty-five days.

For children with a specific interest such as, say, sailing, it is best to get in touch direct with the governing body of the sport, who will supply, at a nominal cost, a list of approved centres. Riding: The British Horse Society, National Equestrian Centre, Kenilworth, Warwickshire, publish a list, price 40p. Pony trekking: Ponies of Britain, Brookside Farm, Ascot, Berkshire, publish a list of centres at 30p. Sailing: Royal Yachting Association, Victoria Way, Woking, Surrey GU21 1EQ, whose list costs 20p.

Photographic acknowledgements

J. Allan Cash, 33, 51, 64, 69, 74, 79, 87, 93, 102, 109;
Peter Baker, 115; British Tourist Authority, 12, 27, 36, 39,
43; Mark Edwards, 19; National Parks Commission, 97;
Derek Pratt (British Waterways Board), 23; Sports
Council, 48; E. W. Tattersall (Countryside Commission),
58; John Walmsley, 120.

If you would like a complete list of Arrow books
please send a postcard to
P.O. Box 29, Douglas, Isle of Man, Great Britain.